∞

Prayer and the Will of God

Other books by Hubert van Zeller
from Sophia Institute Press®:

Holiness for Housewives
How to Find God

Hubert van Zeller

Prayer and the Will of God

SOPHIA INSTITUTE PRESS®
Manchester, New Hampshire

Prayer and the Will of God was formerly published in 1978 by Templegate Publishers, Springfield, Illinois, as a combined edition of *Prayer in Other Words* (Templegate, 1963) and *The Will of God in Other Words* (Templegate, 1964). This 2009 edition by Sophia Institute Press® includes minor editorial revisions.

Sophia Institute Press®
Box 5284, Manchester, NH 03108
1-800-888-9344
www.sophiainstitute.com

Library of Congress Cataloging-in-Publication Data

Van Zeller, Hubert, 1905-1984.
    [Prayer in other words]
    Prayer and the will of God / Hubert van Zeller.
      p. cm.
    Originally published: Springfield, Ill. : Templegate Publishers, 1978. With minor editorial revisions.
    ISBN 978-1-933184-59-3 (pbk. : alk. paper) 1. Prayer — Catholic Church. 2. Christian life — Catholic authors. 3. God (Christianity) — Will. I. Van Zeller, Hubert, 1905-1984. Will of God in other words. II. Title. III. Title: Will of God in other words.
    BV210.3.V36 2009
    248.3'2 — dc22

                       2009026102

09 10 11 12 13 14 10 9 8 7 6 5 4 3 2 1

For Susan, Stephen, John, Paul, Mary:
the Andersons in other words
and
To Mary Vander Vennet
in the hope that she may
come upon it one day

∾

Contents

∞

∽

Prayer and the Will of God

Editor's note: The biblical quotations in the following pages are taken from the Douay-Rheims edition of the Old and New Testaments. Where applicable, quotations have been cross-referenced with the differing names and enumeration in the Revised Standard Version, using the following symbol: (RSV =).

Part 1

∞

Prayer

Chapter 1

∞

Why We Must Pray

Why do people not pray enough? The answer is partly because they do not want to make the effort to begin, and partly because they do not know how to go on once they have begun. A lot of this difficulty would be cleared up if people would only understand that prayer comes from God, is kept going by God, and finds its way back to God by its own power. All we have to do is to lend ourselves to the process as generously as we can, and not put any obstacles in the way.

Our Lord is the light of the world, and by His light we are shown how to start and how to go on. The best way to think of it is to look upon our Lord's prayer as an all-powerful dynamo that sends out spiritual strength day and night, unceasingly. From this dynamo our souls are charged, and when the batteries have gotten run down, we come again and again, every time we pray, to be recharged.

Without prayer we are in darkness, but in God's light we see light.[1]

---

[1] Cf. Ps. 35:10 (RSV = Ps. 36:9).

Our Lord has said that we have not chosen Him but that He has chosen us.[2] It is the same in this matter of prayer. We are not so holy or so clever that we can *make* prayer. Prayer is a grace. Prayer is so spiritual that it has to be made by God. God brings our prayer out of us by pouring His prayer in. We are just the bellows: His is the breath of life. When our Lord speaks of the Spirit breathing and the Light shining, He is speaking of His life in us.

If we share our Lord's life, we must also share His prayer. This is the wonderful thing about being a member of His Church — that we are part of His Body and part of the service He offers to the Father. He draws our service out of us by establishing Himself in our souls. We have the infinite merits of His life, death, and Resurrection to call upon at every moment of our lives. We cannot please God more than by calling upon them in the particular service of prayer.

∞

Or you could put it this way. If you love someone very much, what is it that pleases you most about that person? You will surely answer, "Being loved back." It is knowing that the other person feels as you do; it is seeing in another the same thing that is terribly important to you. Now, God *is* love. What He wants to see in you is the love He has put there. And He wants to see it expressed — He wants it to show. And *that* is why He wants you to pray.

Perhaps you think of prayer as wanting something from God when you pray. Up to a point, this is right: you want mercy, strength to resist temptation, answers to particular petitions, graces of one sort or another. But it would be more true to say that God wants something out of you when you pray. What He wants out of

---

[2] Cf. John 15:16.

you is a generous response to the prayer of His own, which, as we have already seen, He has put there.

He who has created all things, who owns heaven and earth, wants something that you alone among all the millions of human beings who have been born into this world can give. He wants your own, particular, personal, direct, here-and-now service. Nobody else can give it instead of you: it is yours alone to be given to Him alone. Your service of prayer is seen by God as a single thing by itself. You can either give it or refuse it.

By giving it, you give the best that is in you — because it is His own love that you are returning to Him — and by refusing it, you waste the greatest chance that God can offer you. When you pray, you are using your human powers to their highest possible limit — in fact, you are using them *beyond* their highest possible limit because in prayer they are being carried along by grace — and when you have decided to give up prayer, you have thrown away the one really solid support that you can depend upon in this life.

∞

God gets a truly spiritual prayer from the angels and saints in heaven. He gets a mixed sort of prayer from you and me. Our prayer is spiritual (or it would not be prayer at all), but it is also bound up with these fallen natures of ours, which we cannot escape. For as long as we live on this earth, we shall have to be content with a weighted prayer, a prayer that we can never quite handle as we would like, a gritty and earthy prayer that has to be constantly lifted up and sent on its way more directly toward God.

But however weighted down our prayer may be, it is at least a prayer. It is an effort, and has made a start. If we can honestly say we are trying, we can just as honestly say we are praying. So long as I am really trying to please God in my prayer (or in anything else, for that matter), I *am* pleasing Him. All He asks is that I should try to serve Him. The moment I try, I am in fact succeeding. I do not have to feel that I am doing it well, and that my prayer is pleasing God, because feelings are likely to be quite wrong about the goodness or badness of our prayers. All I have to be clear about is that I am making the effort.

Chapter 2

∞

How We Should Pray

After reading what has been said so far, you may feel like someone who has been told how necessary swimming is and then has been thrown into the water without being told how to keep afloat. To know how important prayer is — and religiously, you cannot keep afloat without it — will not be much good to you unless you go on to the next step, which is to learn how to go about it.

Having taken in what is called the principle of prayer, we now have to think about the performance.

Now, whether the performance is an outward one, bringing you together with other people to pray in a church, or whether you are praying on your own, the worship you give must be *yours*. It is person-to-Person. Even a ceremony in which everyone takes part (such as the Mass) is, underneath the printed words, a private conversation between you and God. What is called "liturgical" prayer is God's revelation of Himself made public — a revelation that invites a personal as well as a public return from those who are joining in. As if nobody else were there, God is revealing something of Himself especially to you.

The fact that in public worship other people *are* there makes your response to God all the more pleasing to Him. He wants the members of His Body to be together in prayer and charity — all doing the same thing, but each in his own way. That is why there are churches and congregations. If He wanted a purely private devotion out of us, God would allow us to do all our praying at home. The truth is He wants both: He wants us to pray as part of a crowd because we are united to one another in the family of His Church, and He wants us to pray by ourselves because members of a family can often get closer to their Father when the others are not around.

You will notice that I have called prayer "God's revelation of Himself," which asks you to reveal yourself to Him in return. You may wonder at the word *revelation*, because when you are praying, you do not seem to notice anything of the kind. But a revelation does not always mean a blinding flash, the discovery of an important truth, the understanding of a mystery or a secret. Certainly it means something learned, something unveiled and imparted. When we pray, we come to know God better. We come to see by faith beyond the curtain that hides Him from us. Our knowledge, faith, and love are increased in the act of prayer. It does not happen suddenly, or even noticeably, but it does happen.

Say you were to stand in front of a painting, a masterpiece. If you were ready to take in what you saw, you would gain in knowledge. Your knowledge would make you like the picture. Your liking for the picture would make you understand a little about the artist who painted it. So, altogether you would be a lot better off, in regard to art, from having stood for a while in front of a masterpiece and gazed at it. The perfection of the work would have revealed itself to you.

Apply this to standing before God in prayer. Without having a vision or hearing a divine voice, without perhaps noticing at all what has been going on, you have been taking in something of God. Every time you pray, whether you are aware of the effect it is having upon you or not, you develop in the knowledge and love of God. God so imparts Himself to us in prayer, so "reveals" Himself, that we come away from it with the whole religious side of our natures enlarged and strengthened.

So what it all amounts to is that what God does for us in prayer is infinitely more important than what we do for Him in prayer. We cannot increase His knowledge and love of us in prayer — because He knows us through and through already, and loves with an eternal and infinite love — but He can increase our knowledge and love of Him. This is prayer's particular grace: that we understand more, and therefore want to worship more. In his light we see light, and, seeing, are drawn to praise.

But to go back for a minute to the art gallery, it is obvious that you will not learn much about art, or come to have a liking for it, if you stand in front of the picture with your eyes shut. Or with your eyes open but with your mind closed. You have to look, you have to be ready to understand whatever the picture is supposed to mean. So also in prayer. You have to focus on God. You have to be ready to receive whatever He intends for you.

This is where the practical side of prayer begins — when you ask yourself, "*How* do I focus on God? . . . *How* do I get ready for what He intends? . . . How can I be sure of *what* He intends?" Always remembering that prayer is a matter of faith, and therefore a matter of operating more or less in the dark, we have at least certain lines to go upon which were given us by our Lord Himself. Fortunately, we are not left entirely to ourselves, and to see where our help lies, we must turn to the next chapter.

Chapter 3

∞

Prayer in the Gospels

If we went through the four Gospels with a pencil, marking the places where prayer is mentioned, we would end up with a very long list. The list would be still longer if we included the times when, without mentioning prayer, our Lord speaks about love of His heavenly Father. Love is bound to break into prayer. The Gospels should teach us at least one absolutely clear truth about prayer — namely, that love inspires it, explains it, and crowns it.

Take the example of our Lord Himself. Strictly speaking, because He was united to His heavenly Father at every moment of His life, He had no *need* to pray. That is to say, He had no need to *show* His prayer. The fact that He was one with the Father *was* His prayer. But still He prayed outwardly and in a way that people could follow and understand. Why? Not only because love must burst out into praise, but because human beings had to be told about prayer and had to be shown how love works.

From the Gospels we learn how our Lord prayed in the early morning and late at night, how He prayed before working certain miracles, how He prayed over Jerusalem, how He prayed during the forty days of His fast in the desert, how He prayed when the most important times of His life were approaching, how He prayed for particular people (such as St. Peter, that his faith might not fail, and the Twelve, that they might always be one), how He prayed during the Agony in the Garden and finally during the last hours of His life. All this was praise to the Father but it was also an example to us. If our Lord, who is the head of the Body to which we belong, prayed so much and so often, then we, the members of that Body, must follow His lead.

The lessons to be learned, of course, are that morning and evening are the best times for prayer (because they are usually the quietest times, and it is easier for us to be alone); that we must pray for other people (especially for those who are weak and likely to fall away); that we must pray when we are tempted (and we are often particularly tempted when we are trying to do something really worthwhile for God); that we must pray extra hard before making an important decision or when faced with an important change in our lives (as our Lord prayed before choosing the Twelve, and when entering upon His Passion); and finally when we feel that the end of our life is near.

So nothing could be more practical than the application of our Lord's example to our own individual needs. The Gospels are not written simply to present us with a story; they are for our instruction, for our help, for our advance in love and service and prayer. That is why the best material for prayer is a passage from one or another of the Gospels. Take any incident in our Lord's life, or any paragraph out of our Lord's preaching, and ask yourself how it affects you.

Remember that the Gospels are the word of God, and that He is speaking His word to you. The Holy Spirit does not have to shout at you to make the divine message clear to your soul; you do not have to wait until you hear miraculous voices before you start moving toward God. The inspiration is all there for you in the written word of God. Some bits of the Gospel will appeal to you more than others. God wants them to; He has arranged things like this. Well, make a point of looking out for passages that can become highlights of meaning for you especially. When you come upon a chapter, or even upon a verse or two, that sets something ringing in your soul, keep a firm hold on it, and do not let it go until you have discovered what it is trying to tell you. It has been written for you after all.

It is a tremendous help when you find yourself being addressed personally by the revealed word of God. Not only does it give you confidence, and the feeling that you have been singled out for the love of God, but it also puts you on the alert to find other passages of the same kind. Nothing helps prayer so much as the discovery that the words of God are *alive* — and alive for *you*. Whenever you get this sense of being at home in sacred scripture — and there is nothing silly or unreal about this feeling, because it is exactly the effect the scriptures are meant to have — be careful to follow it up.

The way to follow up such an impulse of grace is not to force your head into a course of biblical study. That might have a terribly cramping effect. No, all you have to do is to ask yourself three very simple questions:

- What does this bit of the story (or this point in our Lord's teaching) tell me about God?

- What does it tell me about myself?

- What does it tell me of the will of God for me?

If you are absolutely honest about answering the second and third question, you will not only be learning a lot of the way of humility and obedience to the divine plan, but you will also be praying. You will be groping toward truth. When you have found out something of your real self, and have accepted the arrangements of God's providence, you will be learning more and more about God Himself. All this will be a form of prayer. It may not be prayer as you see it set down in books, and it may not express itself much in words, but so long as it is a drawing near to truth and love and the infinite goodness of God, it will be prayer all right.

What else do we learn about prayer from the Gospels? Our Lord's example starts us off, telling us that we have got to go ahead and pray. His sermons tell us how to go about it. He does not lay down many rules about prayer (nothing like so many as the books about prayer lay down), but the few He gives us are clear and simple and absolutely necessary. And they can be practiced by all — not only by the experts and saints.

The first thing is to realize that God has a father's love for us and that we must go to Him in confidence and without fear — as affectionate children would go to an affectionate parent. Later in this book, we shall be going through the Our Father, and more will be said about the fatherhood of God. But even if our Lord had never given us the Our Father, He said enough about what our approach should be in prayer to convince us that the father-and-son relationship needed to be understood before anything else.

We are so used to this idea of loving God as a father that we forget how new it was when our Lord preached it to His followers. In the Old Testament, the faithful had praised God in their prayers, had begged for mercy, had promised penance, and had given thanks. But they had not gone very deeply into the idea that God was the God of love. They feared Him as a judge more than they loved Him as a father. Then came our Lord, and the New Testament is full of the *love* of God. God is still a judge, of course, because punishment and pardon have to be dealt out to His creatures by a divine and just Creator, but His justice is that of a devoted parent.

Consider the fabled father who gave scorpions to his children when they asked him for eggs.[3] How could a son love his father if all he got from him was a stone instead of bread? If the son pleaded to be given a fish and was handed a serpent, where would be the love in *that* family? Using these ancient illustrations of home life, deliberately exaggerated so that we should see how impossible would be such a father-and-son relationship, our Lord teaches us to feel at home with God. We are His children and He loves us. That is the first thing to grasp if we are to pray to Him.

Also from the Gospels, much more than from what had been said by the prophets and patriarchs, we get the idea of humility being needed for true prayer. This is shown especially in the parable of the Pharisee and the publican, where the prayer of the ordinary humble sinner is judged better than that of the religious man who is proud, but it is shown, too, where our Lord scolds the kind of pious people who pray out loud in the streets so as to attract attention.[4]

Another thing. "And when you are praying, speak not much as the heathens do," says our Lord, "for they think that in their much speaking they may be heard."[5] Words are all right so long as we

---

[3] Cf. Luke 11:12.

[4] Luke 18:9-14; Matt. 6:5.

[5] Matt. 6:7.

mean them, but words just for the sake of words are not going to please God. He reminds us that there are people who can say, "Lord, Lord" all day long and yet who fail to do God's will.[6] So however holy our words are, they must have more to them than the sound they make. However *many* our prayers are, they must have more to them than mere numbers.

Our Lord also said (not in a sermon this time, but in a talk with a woman who was drawing water) that to worship the Father properly, you had to do so "in spirit and in truth."[7] This, coming on top of what was preached in the Sermon on the Mount, is very important. It means that what really matters in this question of prayer is what goes on in the heart and in the mind. It is the spirit in which we pray that counts. If our spirit is in line with the Holy Spirit — in other words, if we are responding to grace — we are bound to be praying right. The actual phrases we use may be clumsy or may be beautiful; we need not worry about them too much. All we have to worry about is what we intend *inside*. Am I being honest with God, or is my prayer untrue? Is my spirit straight before Him, one with His Spirit, or am I praying according to a crooked spirit of my own?

There are two more states of mind that our Lord particularly wants to see in us when we set ourselves to pray: the first is faith, and the second is the readiness to go on and on. (He also wants us to be at peace with our fellow human beings, forgiving them if they have injured us, but this we are going to deal with when we go through the Our Father.) You have only to think of it for a

---

[6] Cf. Matt. 7:21.
[7] John 4:23.

moment, and you will see that without either belief in the power of prayer or perseverance in its practice, there can be nothing on which your worship rests.

To begin with, then, faith. Faith has a lot of sides to it, and all of them have to find a place in the act of prayer. This is not to say that when you are praying, you have to remind yourself: "I believe that God exists, I believe He can hear my prayer, I trust His promises, I have confidence in the granting of my request, I am sure He is close to me at this moment although He seems to be miles away, I am convinced that what the Church tells me about Him is absolutely true, and I know that everything will be made clear when I get to heaven." If your faith had to work like that, you would end up with a brainstorm. You do not have to make a list of the different ways in which to pray by faith. You simply have to trust completely in God, and throw yourself and your prayer upon divine providence.

Put like that, it ought to be so easy. Yet how many of us have the kind of faith God wants to see in our prayers? Do we honestly believe that God is caring for us at every moment of our lives, and that we have no reason to be anxious about anything at all? Yet it is evidently what He expects. "Be not solicitous for your life," says our Lord in the Sermon on the Mount, "nor for your body . . . Behold the birds of the air, for they neither sow nor do they reap nor do they gather into barns, and your heavenly Father feedeth them. Are not you of much more value than they? . . . Consider the lilies of the field, how they grow . . . and if the grass of the field, which is today and tomorrow is cast into the oven, God doth so clothe, how much more you, O ye of little faith? Be not solicitous, therefore, saying, 'What shall we eat, or what shall we drink, or wherewith shall we be clothed?' For after all these things do the heathens seek. Your Father knoweth that you have need of these things. Seek ye first the kingdom of God and His justice, and all these things shall be added to you."[8] Ask yourself: have I got that kind of faith?

Then there is the famous "faith that moves mountains." Certainly there can be few of us who have that kind of faith, or mountains would actually be moved. If we *had* that kind of faith, we would always — provided we were not praying for the wrong things — find our petitions granted. But at least there is this to be said, that even if we cannot claim to possess that wholehearted trust which does not worry about the future, nor that firmness of belief which works miracles, we have enough faith to enable us to pray. And to pray hard and well. By our baptism we have been given the grace of faith, and nobody can say that the supply of it is too small for the work of prayer. That would be no excuse at all.

And now, lastly, perseverance. There is hardly a mention of prayer in the Gospels that does not hammer upon the need to go on and on and never give up. Our Lord gives the example of a late-night visitor knocking so constantly on the door that the owner of the house at last gets out of bed and comes down.[9] There is the other example of the judge who gives in because the repeated pleading of a woman has worn him down.[10] These are just imaginary cases our Lord chooses, but there are actual incidents as well that tell the same story. The most obvious one to pick out is the occasion when the woman with the sick daughter refused to be shaken off by the apostles, refused even to be silenced by the words of our Lord Himself, which were spoken to test her spirit, and when perseverance was miraculously rewarded.[11]

[8] Matt. 6:31-33.
[9] Luke 11:5-8.
[10] Luke 18:1-5.
[11] Mark 7:24-30.

As if examples and incidents were not enough to prove the point, our Lord preached perseverance when He told His hearers to ask, and seek, and knock in their prayers. Notice the stages: we are urged to ask first of all, and then to continue with our search, and finally to bang on the door until it is opened for us. At each stage, we are given the grace to go on to the next. It means that God wants us to go on praying whether our prayers are answered or not. If our petitions are granted, we make new ones; if they are not granted, there is all the more reason to go praying that they should be.

Those are the main things that should show up in our effort to pray: an understanding of the fatherhood of God, a humble admission of our sinfulness, a truthfulness before God, a living faith and the willingness to persevere. It is all there in the Sermon on the Mount, and notice that our Lord closes His discourse with the description of a man building a house. If the house is built on a foundation of rock, it will stand up to weather and flooding; if it is built on sand, it will collapse.[12] Those who listen to His words and keep them are on solid ground; those who neglect His teaching will fall. It was the same doctrine that He was to teach on the last evening with His apostles before the Passion. "Watch and pray lest you enter into temptation." If we keep on the alert, living up to the lessons He has given us, we are safe. But if we do not watch, and especially if we do not *pray*, we shall find ourselves entering into temptation. And temptation will be too much for us.

[12]Matt. 7:24-27.

Chapter 4

∞

The Our Father

When the disciples asked Him to teach them how to pray, our Lord gave them the pattern of prayer: the Our Father. Besides being a vocal prayer divinely inspired, the Our Father was an instruction *on* prayer. If we take it bit by bit, looking at each of its clauses separately, we shall see that it tells us far more about worship than we would ever learn from books. As our Lord's own prayer, it gives greater glory to God than any other vocal prayer, and as a lesson on how to pray, it gives us all the information we need. Infinite Wisdom is speaking. It is for human minds to take in all they can.

"When you pray, *thus* shall you pray" — this is the sort of thing you must do. Our Lord did not say: "Here are some set phrases arranged in a sequence: learn them off, and recite them aloud to the Father." (Nor indeed had the disciples asked Him for a set prayer they could write down, read over, and say by heart. They had asked, "Lord, teach us how to pray.") Our Lord was giving to his closest friends — and over their shoulders, as it were, to every generation of man until the end of time — the secret of holiness. He was telling them how to worship the Father "in spirit and in truth."

It was as if He was saying: "You want to pray as I do? You want to get into the habit of being united with the Father? You want to learn more about God's will, about His love, about His mercy, about the way He wants you to behave toward Him and toward others? All right. I'll explain how you go about it. You start off by calling upon God as your father and the father of all human beings. Something like this: *Our Father who art in heaven.* Then you think about that for a little while before you move on to the next stage, which is praise . . . And so on. So let us do just that.

Our Father who art in heaven. The *our* means we are not speaking for ourselves alone. We are praying *with* all mankind, and *for* all mankind. This makes the prayer more unselfish. Also, if it is prayed in the name of millions of other souls, it gathers force. It shares in millions of other Our Fathers that are being said all over the world. If it began "My Father who art in heaven," it might be a more private prayer, but it would not have as much charity in it. And charity matters more than privacy. *Our* shows to God that you want to include everyone in your act of love.

The subject of *Father* we have thought about a lot already. But for this matter of prayer, we cannot think about it enough. If the second word of the most important prayer in the whole of creation is *Father* (and in the Latin version, it is the *first* word), then clearly it is something which gives the line on the other clauses that are to come. "Be as a child before God," is what this opening sentence tells us, "and admit your dependence. Come to Him with the whole family of human beings. You are all His children, and He loves each one of you as a father would love an only child."

"Who art in heaven" — to show that we, as creatures of a lower order, bow before His majesty. He lives in heaven, we on earth. But in case this should make us think of Him as up in the clouds, far away from the world He has created, we must know that He is very much present here on earth as well. If He wanted to be thought of as a distant master, running the world by remote control, He would not have called Himself a father. A father is someone who is ordinarily at home.

Hallowed be Thy name. Having addressed yourself to God — that is, having explained that you want to get in touch with the Father — you go on to praise His name. *Hallowing* means giving glory or worship. The Father's name, our Lord's name, the Holy Spirit's name: it is all one name. You give praise before you start asking for things. God knows well enough what it is that you need, and that in a minute you will be asking for it, but He wants you to begin your prayer on a note of homage. It is like a father telling his son not to snatch. Later on, the son can pester, but he is much more likely to get what he pesters for if he is polite at the outset. Also it is possible to be mistaken about petition, whereas you cannot go wrong about praise. So get your praising done first, and be sure that you mean it every bit as much as you mean your petitions.

Thy kingdom come. This carries on from what has just been prayed, showing that the kingdom of God must come first and the world of man second. Notice, too, that it is a kingdom and not a throne: there are people in it. So again there is this notion of all being together in the one prayer, under the one King, sharing the one love in charity with others. "When we pray," says St. Cyprian,[13] "it

---

[13] St. Cyprian (c. 200-258), Bishop of Carthage and martyr.

is not for one soul but for all souls, because we all are one. God teaches us peace, concord, unity. He bears us all in one Person, and wills that each should pray for all." If everyone in the kingdom of God on earth took this to heart, we would be living in an ideal community. But our earthly community is not ideal, so we pray "Thy kingdom come."

∞

Thy will be done on earth as it is in heaven. Once we have adored God as King of heaven and earth, we move on naturally to the position where we fall in with His ruling on earth with the same sort of obedience to His will which is given by the angels and saints in heaven. We need not pretend that we are as good at this act of submission as the angels and saints, but at least we can pray that God's will may meet with no resistance. Anyway, we mean to accept whatever providence arranges.

Now, the more this state of mind is kept up, the more glory we give to God and the holier we become. We take everything in our stride because we know that everything is somehow allowed for in the plan of God. If we can get into the habit of meeting every difficulty, every disappointment, every pleasure, and every problem with this clause of the Our Father, we are in a fair way toward reliving our Lord's life. All the time we shall be echoing His words: "I came not to do my own will but the will of Him who sent me . . . not what I will but what Thou wilt."[14] There can be no true holiness, and no true prayer, where the will of God is deliberately resisted. Our first duty as religious people, as Christians, is to try to live up to this fourth sentence of the Our Father. It is the hinge on which all the others turn. Examine yourself on it, do your best to

[14]Cf. John 6:38; Matt. 26:39.

use it so often that it becomes instinctive, and make a point of showing in practice that you mean it.

Give us this day our daily bread. Now, having got your will into line with God's, you can start asking for things. This is not simply a piece of good manners — accepting the bread-and-butter before helping yourself to cake — but a piece of spiritual wisdom. Once the soul has learned something of the will of God, there is no danger of asking for the wrong things. You find yourself asking for the kind of bread that God wants you to have. The purpose of prayer is not to bring God's will down to your level so that you may get what you want. The purpose of prayer is to lift your will to God's level so that you may get what *He* wants.

Does this sound complicated? Well, put this petition in other words, and it will read something like this: "Lord, there are many things I would like to have, and quite a lot that I seem to *need*, but because I am a selfish, greedy person, I am probably fooling myself into thinking them so important. So I ask that You may judge what is best for me, and give me the things that have on them the stamp of Your will." Such a way of looking at it should not put us off from begging for all sorts of unlikely things that we may perhaps not need but which we would very much like to have. God will decide whether they are good for us or not, and in the meantime, we can go ahead and ask.

Obviously the most important things to ask for are graces and virtues and the strength to resist sin — the greatest of all graces coming to us in the daily bread of Holy Communion — but we do not have to ask only for the best things. A child does not ask his father only for shelter, education, and support — in fact, these important things are usually taken for granted between father and son — but is perfectly free to ask for a bicycle or for money to go to a movie.

And that is enough for the moment about the prayer of petition because there will be more on the subject in another chapter.

∞

Forgive us our trespasses as we forgive those who trespass against us. The rule is perfectly clear: in order to expect pardon, you must grant it. To show that no prayer can please God where there is a feud going on, our Lord says in the Sermon on the Mount that if, in the act of offering sacrifice to God, you suddenly remember that a person has a complaint against you (and that supposedly you have a complaint against him), then you must leave the altar and make peace before going on with the act of worship. Injuries must be straightened out by forgiveness, or there is no prayer.

Again we seem to have a picture of children squabbling and being forgiven by their father only on condition that they agree to drop their resentments and make friends again. What we have to ask ourselves is this: Am I slow to ask God's pardon for my sins — and if so, is it because I am not forgiving enough myself? I must get the idea of mercy right from both sides: God's and mine. I must look out for chances of making peace with others, forgiving them in my heart at once if they have wronged me; I must also be quick to ask pardon of God the moment I know that I have wronged Him.

The trouble is, I misunderstand God and am far too slow with my acts of contrition. Do I think of Him as a stern parent who is likely to get angry, who has to be kept in a good mood, whose children have to walk on tiptoe and sit up straight? Do I think of Him as touchy, given to misunderstandings, liable to hold it against me that I have failed so often in the past?

Now, it is important that I should get all this right. Otherwise I shall never be able to go to God when I am in difficulties, return to Him when I have sinned, pray to Him properly, or feel at ease with him. I must know from the start that whatever other fathers are like, this Father loves me all the time and can never change. Not only does He always want me near Him, always want the best possible thing for me, always want me to call upon Him for help when I am sad or in trouble, *but He always goes on loving me even when I have sinned against Him and am hanging back from repentance.* Did I know this? Probably not, because the books do not *say* it much. But it is true — theologically true. It all turns on two facts: first, that God is love, and second, that God cannot change.

So it would be a complete mistake for me to imagine that I have somehow got to calm down the just wrath of a grieved parent, or that I have to wait a while for his anger to cool and for his sadness at my failure to lessen with the passing of time. God and His love are one thing, and that one thing never alters. God loves me when I have not sinned, but He loves me also when I have. He would not be God if He stopped loving me. If He *could* stop loving me, it would mean that God was divided — that His divinity was in one part of Him and His love in another, and that He could go on being divine while deciding at the same time to stop loving. It would be heresy to hold this.

But for goodness' sake, do not get the doctrine wrong. God does not love you to sin (that is the last thing He wants you to do), but He does love you although you sin. What it amounts to is that His love is there, waiting for you, and that even if you are in such a bad mood that you refuse to ask for pardon, He is still just as ready to give it to you when you do. The instant you have responded to grace, humbling yourself and admitting your fault, you are fully back again in His love as though you had never left it. In your obstinacy, it was not His love that had left you, but your love that had left him

If you try to understand how this works, you come to a much truer knowledge of God and of His love for you. We have just seen that with your repentance the father-and-son relationship is perfectly restored. Not a cloud to darken it. Now, it is not as though God is saying, "I won't think about it; I'll forget it. We both know you have offended me, but we'll pretend it never happened. We must start again, and see if we can't get along better." God is not that kind of father, the let's-pretend kind. Infinite Wisdom cannot either "forget" or "remember": everything is spread out there before Him in His eternity.

Nor can He try an experiment. He cannot say: "This getting along better together may or may not work out. I don't know. We'll simply have to see. We must do our best." God knows everything all the time, and it would be silly to think of Him either as blotting things out of His memory or veiling His knowledge of the future. What He blots out is our guilt, not His knowledge of our guilt. He is not blindfolded about the future; it is only we who cannot be sure what response we are going to give to the grace that will certainly be there for us to use.

Now, does not this make God's love all the more wonderful? The perfection of friendship lies not in pretending that nothing had ever gone wrong, or ever would go wrong again, but in being always open to full friendship, whatever happens. It should be a great help to know that God never bears a grudge against a sinner, is never suspicious, and never loses confidence in the sinner's ability to return to Him.

No question here of God's taking a nice mild view of sin. God is infinite goodness, and sin is the dead opposite of goodness. God could no more belittle sin than He could belittle love. It is just because God is love that sin is unlove — is rebellion, is pride, is evil. If sin hurt *us* only, and were not an offense against God, it would not matter quite so much. But because it attacks the infinite goodness and love of God, sin is the vilest thing in the world.

So when we talk about God's "hating" sin, we should not think of God's feeling bitter about it, as a man might loathe something that got in the way of his plans or of his happiness. Nothing can get in the way of God's plan *or* of His happiness. God's will cannot be altered by human beings, nor can God's happiness be upset by anything that man can do. No, God is not shocked, soured, or stung to malice by the sins committed against Him. These are simply human moods and instincts which it would be wrong to think that God could feel. The evil of sin lies in the rejection of God, not in any feelings that it stirs.

In the Passion, our Lord's feelings were allowed to suffer infinite pain, and it was because of our sins that this happened, but we may not believe that we can, by our sins, cause sadness to God, for He is now in the eternal bliss of heaven. If we could sadden God, it would mean that He was even now at the mercy of man. If the Holy Trinity were not safe from the malice of man, from your sins and mine, it would be impossible to claim for the three Persons that They enjoy infinite happiness in the love of one another.

So it is quite a wrong way of looking at it to think of God in heaven gazing reproachfully down upon the human race and saying, "I feel terribly hurt when these people sin, and if they go on like this, I won't love them any more." The right way to look at it is to think of Him as saying, "I want these people to be good because I love them, and when they are good, they are being like me. When they are committing sin, they are being the very opposite of me. When in sin, they are not worthy of my love. But my love is so great that, worthy or not, they can always count on it."

Lord, forgive us our debts as we also forgive our debtors. We have sinned, but we count on Your mercy. We do not want to continue in our sin. Lord, make us worthy of Your great love.

∞

And lead us not into temptation. Get used to the idea that, all through your life, temptation will never be far away. Since the Fall of man, it is part of life itself, and only our Lord and His blessed Mother have been proof against it. But even they had to endure its heat.

Temptation is not sin; it is only the air in which sin is born. Temptation is the climate that makes sin feel at home. If you keep away from the occasions of sin, filling your lungs with air that is purified by grace, the evil that lies in temptation will not infect you. In fact, you will see in it a chance of practicing self-control.

St. James goes so far as to say that we should count it all joy when we fall into various temptations.[15] Why — if temptation is so dangerous to our souls? Because without the test of temptation, the strength of virtue would not show up. It is temptation that throws the soul back upon God's grace as the only way of escape.

So it is only when you go looking for the foul air, or when you choose to walk about in it when its clouds roll in upon you, that you can no longer be sure of making use of God's protecting grace. The grace will be there all right, but in your divided state of mind, you may not want to be protected by it.

Lord, lead me away from temptation. Let me not risk an occasion of sin. When opportunities of offending You come upon me, give me warning in time and show me the way out of them.

---

[15]James 1:2.

∞

But deliver us from evil. Amen. Just as there are two kinds of temptation (the kind we cannot escape altogether but do not want, and the deliberate kind we lay ourselves open to), so there are two kinds of evil (although same would say there are a thousand kinds of evil because there are a thousand kinds of devil in us, each one greedy for its own particular kind of satisfaction). Anyway, there are two main ones as far as committing sin is concerned, and care must be taken not to confuse the two, or we find ourselves tangled up in scruples.

The easiest way to see the difference between mortal and venial sin is to compare it with the sort of quarrels that happen between friends. Two people disagree. One of them may say to himself as he walks away from the scene of the argument, "We have had a row, but it won't make any difference to our friendship. I don't want to break things up. I am all for getting my own way now, but by tomorrow it will have blown over and we'll be getting along together as before." The other one may say to himself, "Well, that's finished it. I never want to see him again. Look around for someone else." Venial sin would be like the first man's attitude toward the break: it is a thing of the moment, and can be healed in no time. Mortal sin is like the second way of looking at it: the relationship has collapsed, and there is a turning away that is expected to be final.

Lord, deliver us from evil. Deliver us from both kinds, venial and mortal sin, but especially from the evil of mortal sin. Compared with the evil of mortal sin, all the other evils that we can think of (disease, war, poverty, loneliness, concentration camps, death) are not so very serious after all. In every human distress, the soul can still love God, but in the evil of mortal sin, the soul is dead — although even now, putting it at its worst and supposing that we have deliberately committed a mortal sin, we should know that there is still a way back. If a friend can say, "I want nothing more to do with him," and then change his mind, he can ask his friend to forgive him and put things right; the two can get along again as though nothing had happened. The quarrel, with its narrow escape, may even make the guilty one more grateful than he was before, more thoughtful, more careful about not losing his friend's affection. It will certainly make him sorry for having failed the other person and turned against him.

Deliver us from evil, Lord, and we will try to come back with a humble, penitent, and grateful heart. If Your mercy were not infinite, and if Your grace were not stronger than our wickedness, this last clause of the Our Father would not have been given us. The one great thought that we can take away with us from these notes about the Our Father is the thought of Your never-failing mercy. You have been a merciful Father in redeeming us from Original Sin. You have been a merciful Father in forgiving us again and again for our actual sins. Our Father, we trust in Your mercy. Amen.

Chapter 5

∞

Distracted Prayer

If you have gotten this far in the book, you are likely saying to your-self something like this: "Yes, I know. It ought not be difficult to pray. And when I am stuck, I can read over the Our Father slowly, praying about each sentence as it comes along. I can do the same to the Hail Mary or to the words of the Mass. But the plain fact is my mind wanders off every time I pray, and unless I am rapping out prayers like a machine-gun, I cannot be sure that I am doing any praying at all. And the worst of it is that these prayers which rattle along as fast as my tongue can speak them do not seem to mean very much. They become automatic. *How can I pray without distractions?*"

The answer is very simple: you cannot pray without distrac-tions. Except our Lord and our Lady, nobody ever has. You can pray without deliberately choosing to distract yourself, but you cannot pray for long without unwanted distractions coming in and apparently spoiling your prayer. The word *apparently* must be looked at here because the harm done to prayer by distractions that are not deliberate is only apparent. The real value of the prayer remains even when the flow of talk to God is interrupted by other voices that you are trying to shut out.

Prayer and the Will of God

Take an example from everyday life. You put on a long piece of music that you mean to hear right through to the end. You lean forward and listen. But while you are settling in and enjoying it, a door bangs or a telephone rings or someone shouts at you from the garden. Now, these noises may spoil your enjoyment of the music, but they do not stop it from playing. They distract your attention, but only if you decide to see who has banged the door, called up on the telephone, or shouted from outside do you voluntarily switch your mind away from the sounds you had set out to hear. A deliberate distraction does, of course, spoil the prayer, but it would have to be as deliberate as turning off the music. So long as you are still trying to pray, it is the same as still trying to listen to the music; you pay as little attention as possible to the noises that are going on around you, knowing that the noises of themselves cannot stop the music from playing.

This means that when you are praying, you do not have to keep reminding yourself that you *are* praying or the prayer stops. When a distraction comes, you should try to call your thoughts back by telling God once again what you have set yourself to do. "Lord, I am supposed to be praying, and I have been thinking of other things. Please get me on to thinking of You again."

But if you were expected to repeat all during your prayer, "I am now saying my prayers, I am now saying my prayers, I am now saying my prayers," you would only be thinking about yourself and not about God. The fact that you mean to pray is quite enough to keep the important part of the prayer going. It is like taking a trip by air. You do not have to repeat all the time you are in the plane, "I am going somewhere by air" — as if the engine would stop if you forgot to. In prayer, you mean to mount into the sky of God's love, and you do not come down again until the journey is over.

So the real trouble about distractions is not that they wreck the prayer from God's point of view, but that they discourage you and get you to think about yourself. Try not to let your prayer go round and round in circles with you as the center of it. Your prayer is meant to go out from you toward God. The more you try to love Him and forget about yourself, the better. Distractions do not stop you from loving God in your prayer, but thinking about yourself does. Even though you will never be able to leave all thought of yourself behind when you pray — because, after all, it is *you* who are praying — you should try to make the thought of God come first.

One good thing about distractions, whether they take the form of thinking about yourself or about anything else, is that they make you humble. After a prayer that has been full of distractions, you feel you are, so far as the service of God goes, a pretty miserable specimen. The question now is what effect will this have? If it discourages you from going on with praying, it means that you have failed in the test (and that you *are* a pretty miserable specimen). If it makes you say, "This shows how useless I am at prayer, but God can get me to pray better if I give Him half a chance by responding more to His grace," then it means that the test has worked and that you are learning to depend less upon yourself than upon God.

Besides, what would happen if you could always pray without distractions? You would feel you were two-thirds a saint already. You would say, "This is easy; I needn't bother about it anymore." You would think yourself enormously superior to those unfortunate souls whose prayer was nothing but one distraction after another. In other words, you would be the Pharisee, and your beautifully undistracted prayer would not be nearly so pleasing to God as the muddled, creaking, stuttered, disjointed prayer of the publican.

Another point worth thinking about while we are on this subject of distractions is that wherever the novelty of a thing wears off, you are bound to get a rather humdrum and stale performance. Seeing an adventure film for the first time, you get a great thrill, but if you saw it day after day for a month, you would get no thrill at all. Now, in the first place, you do not pray in order to get thrills but in order to praise God. But even if getting thrills was one of the main things about prayer, *they would simply not come*. So, although it would be wrong to pray in a slapdash sort of way, letting your prayer go stale by sheer carelessness, you must remember that anything which you do regularly, and which you have come to know well and which is now a settled habit, cannot have the feeling of freshness about it that it may have had at first.

Perhaps you may wonder why, if it is not meant to last, God allows you to have that sense of freshness in the beginning. "Doesn't it only lead to disappointment?" you may ask. "And wouldn't it be better if devotion had not come my way in the first place? I would then have known what I was in for — a heavy sort of prayer that feels like a waste of time." The answer to that one is roughly this: we human beings are such selfish creatures that if God did not give us a liking for prayer's consolations (the enjoyment of doing something rather special, the satisfaction of getting along rather well, the sheer pleasure of being in His presence undisturbed), we would probably not pray at all. God draws us by what the books call "sensible devotion" (which means the nice warm glow that sometimes comes along with grace) so that we should make a fixed and faithful practice of what was just a pleasurable experience.

Incidentally, He does the same, you will find, when He wants us to get in the way of practicing charity. To serve the sick, to give things to the poor, to be helpful to old people: such acts of kindness make us feel fine when we do them for the first time. But they get stale, and then we are all the more faithful and charitable *because* they feel so stale. The first feelings, you see, do not matter so much as the settled desire. And where you have a settled desire, you seldom have exciting feelings. True charity, which is serving God and serving others, can be quite without excitement. In the matter of charity, it is direction that counts — pointing your love toward God.

The question to get back to every time is *why are we praying?* Are we praying to please God or to please ourselves? It ought not to be too hard for us to answer this question in the way God wants it answered. And again (because, in the long run, it amounts to the same thing) *why are we practicing charity?* Are we serving others to please God or to please ourselves? Our aim should be to pray not because we love prayer but because we love God, to serve others not because we love serving but because we love God. In doing each of these things, praying and serving, we shall find ourselves falling short of the ideal. Provided we keep aiming at the ideal, we need not be discouraged at falling short. Of course, in our prayers we shall catch ourselves being more anxious to get things out of God than to let Him get things out of us. Of course, in our works of charity we shall catch ourselves being more eager to impress with our service than to please with our charity. But these are just distractions to be brushed aside. All the time we are really trying to focus on God.

∞

By way of rounding off this chapter, here is an illustration that may help to explain the workings of distractions both in works of prayer and in works of charity. Someone is taking a close-up photograph of you with a flash. In the sudden bright light from the camera, what do you see? You do not see either the camera or the bulb. You are, for the moment, blinded by the flash. But the camera has seen *you*, and has recorded what it wanted to record. Now when, by prayer, you look into the light and the love of God, you do not see what you might expect to see. The light is too strong for the eyes of your soul, and you do not see anything at all. But God has accepted the direction of your gaze, and it is His side of the business that matters. You must be content to leave the photographing to Him, the developing and printing to Him, the success of the finished copy to Him. All that is wanted of you is that you keep still and try to be natural.

Chapter 6

∞

Unanswered Prayer

If distractions and the feeling that our prayers are no use make up the chief test of our prayer, there are other things as well that come in to add to its difficulty and show its quality. These mostly have to do with the prayer of petition and how it fits in with the plan of God. As we have already seen, God wants us to ask for what we want and to go on asking. Well, the first problem is: Why? He knows what we want; He knows what we are going to ask for; He knows whether He is going to grant our request or refuse it. So why do we have to make prayers of petition? Much simpler not to bother.

But it is not always laziness that is at the back of this objection. Sometimes it is a mistaken kind of virtue. It is the trust-to-luck state of mind that disguises itself as pure faith. Put into words, it comes out something like this: "God in His wisdom has known from all eternity what is best for me. I trust in His providence. It would show a lack of faith on my part, and also a lack of generosity, if I trusted in my own judgment and prayed for my own intention. Surely it is more perfect not to pray for anything but to leave it all to God." This would be to make a great mistake, and would show a complete misunderstanding of both prayer and the nature of God's providence. So we must look at it closely and try to see how the prayer of petition works. If we do not grasp the truth of it, we shall have a first-class excuse for never saying any prayers at all.

For explanation, let us get back once again to the idea of the fatherhood of God. God has certain things in store for us which He knows we need and which He means to give us. But He means to give them only on condition that we ask for them. So he fills our minds with a desire for these things and gives us the grace to turn our desire into a prayer for them. A human father does much the same in dealing with his children. "I'll take them out for a day on the river," he says to himself, "but they must come and ask me for it." Then he talks about rivers and boats, and the children come clamoring to be taken out for the day. But, of course, if the children do not ask, even though they may want it, the party is off. It is up to the children to ask. It is up to us to pray.

The point to remember is that our petitions do not *change* God's mind for Him; they help in carrying out God's mind in the way that He has planned to carry it out. We must not think that our petitions come as a surprise to God — as though God did not *quite* know what we were hoping for and was waiting to be told. All along, billions of years before we were born, our future request has been known to Him. In eternity it was already there, being thought of by God, until at a certain moment in time, He slipped an idea into our human heads and eventually we have come out with it in the form of prayer.

"But even so," you might say, "this only accounts for the prayers that are answered. What about the prayers that are turned down? He must have inspired them, too, and if He did not mean to answer them, why did He inspire them? Wouldn't it have been better to let us forget about praying for things that there would never be any chance of our getting?"

The explanation runs along two lines. First, God is praised by any petition we make to Him in prayer — whether it is one that will be granted or not. So long as we are not praying for something that is downright wrong (success in a robbery, for instance, or an accident to someone we dislike), the mere fact that we are turning to Him for what we want is a sign that we trust and depend on Him. We know whom to go to; we are treating Him as a child treats his father; it gives Him glory.

So the prayer is not wasted if we happen to ask for something that God has no intention of granting. He takes it at its true value, an act of love and worship, even though it comes to nothing from our point of view.

Second, when we pray for something and God does not give it to us, we get something better instead. So, from our point of view, it *does* come to something after all — even though we may not be able to see it like that. God lets us ask for things that are not so good because He knows that we often do not feel inclined to ask for the things that are really good. Well, we pray about these not-so-good intentions and they do not come off, but all the time in heaven they are being turned into much better intentions that *do* come off. A child who sees a bright coin next to a dreary-looking check will ask for the shining bright coin. The father, who knows that the check is worth far more, puts the check in the bank for the child, and does not grant the coin. One day the child will know that this is a better arrangement, but in the meantime complains that his requests are not granted. We should not complain that our prayers are not granted; they are heard all right. They are answered in God's way. We are never losers in prayer.

Another problem that has to do with the prayer of petition is this one: "What happens when two people are praying for the same thing which they can't both have? Is the person who prays harder always bound to win? If not, what is the point of praying during a war for victory? Yet it often happens in history that the harder-praying side loses, and the godless armies have it all their own way." Yes, this is a real difficulty until you look at the business from on top, from God's angle. Seen from down below, with only the here-and-now results to go by, there seems to be a lot of unfairness about the ways in which prayers are heard. But if you try to take God's point of view, you will see that when two people, or two armies, are praying for one thing, He sees what is going to be best for both of them in the long run, and He gives them that. It may be that one or another of them needs punishment, so that one's prayer brings the grace of correction instead of a grace that would be used badly and so bring along more suffering. Suffering, correction, punishment: these things look different when you see them as God sees them.

What has just been said is not an argument for praying less — on the principle that if God is going to reward your prayer with suffering, you had better pray as little as possible — but for praying more. God, looking down from heaven at the greater effort you are putting into your prayer, gives you a clearer view of the situation as it appears to *Him*. Your prayer brings you closer not only to His love but also to His wisdom and knowledge; you begin to see beyond your own little intentions and requests, and at last the bigger questions of suffering and true happiness are opened out to you. You never *lose* by praying — even if the grace it brings to you is not the one you want.

∞

Now, here is another thing. It may be that God has given you the urge to pray for a particular intention, and you have got the urge wrong. Say He suggests to your mind that you should pray for peace, and you do pray for peace — but for your own idea of peace. God is not going to give you the peace of idleness, which would be bad for you, but He gives you peace of conscience instead.

This sort of thing happened in the case of King David, who was urged to pray for a house. He did pray — hard — for a house. But he prayed for a house made of stone and cedar, when all along God meant a "house" in the sense of a family that would go on from generation to generation until finally our Lord would be born of it. David's prayer for a building was rewarded better than he knew. God is not to be blamed when we jump to conclusions, and put our own meaning upon the urges He grants us.

Often God gives us the inspiration to pray for a particular thing, and we do for a bit but then get tired of it and give up. Is God to be blamed because He does not grant our request, the request He Himself has prompted, at once? Even if what we ask for is something obviously very good, like the grace to overcome a bad habit of swearing, we have to go on asking for it. If we stop asking for it, and do not make use of the grace that comes to us, we cannot expect a full answer to our prayer.

Take an example. A boy asks his father if he may stay up late to work for an exam. The father tells his son that he may do this every night until the exam, but that he must ask again if there is another exam later on. The boy's request has been answered, but if he uses the time for watching television, the father cannot be blamed for not renewing the permission. In the same way, the permission is not granted unless the request is renewed.

So we have to go on asking, and we have to back up our petition by making a right use of what we get. If God said yes straight off, He would not have the satisfaction of receiving our repeated prayer. If God went on saying yes when we had no intention of living up to what we were asking for, He would be scattering graces uselessly. It would be both a waste of prayer on our part to ask for something we did not mean to use, and a waste of grace on God's part to give something that was doing no good.

Let us now see what conclusions may be drawn from all of this. Go on making your petitions to God, but do be honest about them. You are dealing with grace and love, not with magic. Do not expect to be miraculously cured of a vice if you do not mean to practice the opposite virtue. Go on and on asking in faith and trust and love, but do not be discouraged if your prayer is not answered in the form you expect. There may be reasons that you do not know about which quite alter the situation as God sees it. And He sees it as it really is. God sees all around the subject, and you do not. (Back for a second to the illustration of the father and the day on the river: the father may refuse the request because he knows it is going to rain, or because he has seen a leak in the boat, or because the children happen to be coming down with measles, only they do not know it.) Lastly, join your petition with the prayer of our Lord, knowing that if you are praying in His name, you are doing two good things at once: you are bound to be pleasing the Father, and you cannot be asking for anything that will do you or anyone else harm.

Chapter 7

∞

Fruitful Prayer

You may remember, from two chapters back, the illustration about someone taking your photograph by flashbulb camera. Now that the effects of prayer are to be looked at, this illustration will again come in useful. You must have noticed that after the photograph has been taken, you go on for a few minutes seeing little circles of light wherever you look. Well, that is what should happen after your prayer has been made. You may not see much *during* your prayer, but afterward and *because* of your prayer, you come to see more and more of God's light wherever you look.

The saints are those who see God's creation as swimming in His light. They see His light dancing on quite ordinary everyday things; their decisions are made according to His light; their sufferings and joys are unfolded in His light; they work, make friends, eat, go to bed, and get up under the steady beam of God's light.

In the case of you and me, who are not saints, there is not a steady beam that we can see, but at least a certain amount of light is the reward of our prayer. This is not to say that every time we pray, we come away seeing God's will more clearly, or that, for the next ten minutes, everything seems to have a halo around it. It is not at all like that.

What happens is that our faith is strengthened by every prayer we make, and with faith we view the world differently and the whole of life differently. There is nothing miraculous or exciting about it. It is simply the result of having been nearer to God for a bit. We get to look at the world and at life through His eyes. If we do not pray, we look at the world and life only through our own, and we are apt to see things wrong.

Our Lord said in the Sermon on the Mount that His followers were "the light of the world."[16] This was because they were walking in His light. So long as we live in His light, we see light. He has said so, and it must be true. He tells us that we must walk while we have the light[17] — because then we are bound to be walking with Him and toward the Father. Again in the Sermon on the Mount (read it, because it contains nearly all our Lord's teaching and is only three short chapters in St. Matthew's Gospel), He explains how everything depends on seeing things right. "The light of thy body is thine eye," he says, "and if thine eye be single, thy whole body shall be full of light. But if thine eye be evil, thy whole body shall be in darkness."[18] Now the way to get this "single eye" that our Lord speaks of and which makes us full of light is to *pray*. The saints have it all the time; we have it only in spells. But the more we pray, the longer we have it, and the more we see, the more wonderful the light.

When (to change the subject for a minute) Veronica was rewarded for her generosity by having the likeness of our Lord's face

[16]Matt. 5:14.
[17]Cf. John 12:35.
[18]Cf. Matt. 6:22-23.

clearly marked upon her veil, she was at the same time being taught a tremendous truth. It was a truth that the whole incident was designed to teach to us. By looking with faith and love at the face of Christ (which is what we are trying to do when we pray), we come to see the imprint of our Lord's features on everyone and everything. It is like seeing the circles of light when the flash has done its work. You may be sure that Veronica, having seen our Lord so close up and having taken away with her the first reproduction of His sacred face, would for the rest of her life look upon her fellow creatures with a new vision. Especially in the features of the suffering, the sick, the poor, the persecuted, she would have seen the likeness of Jesus, to which her veil bore witness.

So you see, it is only indirectly that you can judge the quality of your prayer. Its fruitfulness is known to God alone. It is done for Him, and He alone can tell its value. All you can have to go upon is a few general effects — almost byproducts. If your prayer is going as it should, you ought to be growing in kindness to others, in self-control, in obedience, in patience under suffering. You should be growing, too, in humility, but as this is a virtue that you cannot be expected to see — because it is more a virtue which you see *by* than which you see — it is not much good talking about it here.

Among the more certain signs of a prayer-life that is moving in the right direction is a general prayerfulness outside actual prayer-time. If you find yourself turning to God when there is nothing much else going on, it is a good sign. If you turn to God instinctively when you are in a tight spot, it is a good sign. If you feel drawn to stop on in His presence after Holy Communion, making longer thanksgivings, it is a good sign. If you like trying to pray instead of just daydreaming when you are on a long drive or when you are sick or when you are a long time getting to sleep, it is a good sign. This is called *recollectedness*, and the more you feel attracted to recollection, the more you should know this is a grace from God as well as a proof that you are in the right way. It is a grace to be acted on and developed. It gives great glory to God and is the most solid security in a world of great uncertainty.

Another confirmation, or indirect sign of its fruitfulness, occurs when your prayer becomes less fussy. Too many words, too many elaborate resolutions, too many careful examinations: these things clutter up prayer and get in the way of the directness that God wants to see in our progress toward Him. "In spirit and in truth" — to which might reverently be added, "in simplicity and peace."

We cannot worship God if we are in a fever of complication and agitation. Instinctively we guess that our Lady's prayer was calm and simple and unworried about itself. It was not in a storm that the word of God came to Elijah, but in the soft breathing of the air.[19] We like to stir up a great commotion because it is more exciting. We like to hear the rumble of thunder and the crackling of lightning against the rocks; we like to stand in a high wind and feel the sting of the rain on our faces. But this is movie stuff. These are just fireworks compared with the steady glow of the love of God.

See how simple, direct, and unthrilling is the prayer of the blessed in heaven. Nothing but "Holy, holy, holy, Lord God of Hosts!" No circus tricks — something that anyone can say. See how simple is the canticle of praise that is chanted all day at Lourdes in honor of our Lady: "*Ave, ave, ave,* Maria." Remember such prayers as "Alleluia" and "Amen" and "*Fiat.*" Nothing could

[19] 3 Kings 19:11-13 (RSV = 1 Kings 19:11-13).

be simpler than the prayers inspired by the Holy Spirit. The more our prayers get to be like that, the surer we can be that we are not wasting our time in prayer.

From being unanxious about the workings of our prayer, we should grow to be unanxious about the workings of life as a whole. Our own life, and the life of the world: God has charge of both, and can be left to take care of what is His. When you get down to it, you discover that love is the explanation of everything. God *loves* the world and every soul in it. Why should we break our heads worrying about either our own future or the future of the world? To fear the break-up of the world because man happens to have hit upon a weapon of destruction is just plain silly, is a lack of faith. As if the world could come to an end behind God's back, before He was ready for it, before mankind had been brought to the point God had planned it should reach.

Our prayer should let us see these things in their overall setting, in the setting of divine providence. Once granted that God loves the universe He has created, and once granted that He loves you just as you are in the middle of it, He is not going to forsake it when it runs into a bit of difficulty, and He is not going to forsake you either. Prayer leads to dependence, trust, calm.

Above all, of course, prayer leads to charity toward others. This is put so clearly and sharply in the first letter of St. John that when we come upon the text suddenly, we wonder how we can ever make a mistake about it again. "If you do not love your neighbor whom you see, how can you love God, whom you do not see?"[20] Prayer acts as a searchlight, playing close up on the faces of our neighbors and showing us who they really are under their make-up and their disguises and their masks. Who are they? They are the

[20]Cf. 1 John 4:20.

representatives of God. When we recognize them, we recognize Him. When we extend our charity to them, we are giving our charity to Him. It is as straightforward as that. But we see it so only in the measure that we pray. Prayer, in other words, is the solution to our problem.

Part 2

The Will of God

Chapter 8

Understanding God's Will

There can hardly be a better practice in the spiritual life than that of meeting everything as an expression of the will of God. Phrases such as "if God wills" and "it must be the will of God" and "may God's will go with you" come naturally to the devout. People in certain traditions of Christian life say these things all day long and mean them. God's will becomes for them the standard of everyday decisions and the background against which life happens.

Nothing furthers the supernatural point of view so effectively as the cultivation of such a habit. It can be seen as an extension of the Our Father, as an identification with the disposition of Christ, as the application of "I came not to do my own will, but the will of my Father who is in heaven" to our own human concerns. It can be made to sum up the whole of our Christian service. But "God's will" is not just a magic formula, a password that opens all the gates, a label to be stuck onto luggage that need not be thought about for the rest of the journey. God's will, in other words, is not a superstition.

God's will: it can mean so much — and so little. We accept as God's will the outbreak of a revolution; the breaking of a dam, which means the destruction of homes and harvests and lives; the loss of a leader or of someone we have loved personally. We accept also as God's will a tiresome interruption, the missing of a train, an obstinate tap, an alarm that fails to go off. There is nothing wrong in accepting such circumstances as manifestations of God's will — indeed we should train ourselves to do so — but we must be careful to avoid the misconceptions that would rob the exercise of its value. Even granted that we really mean what we say when we hail an event as God's will, it is important that we should mean what is right.

In the first place, it is a mistake to imagine that the disastrous is the most fitting occasion for the doctrine's application. The implication would be that God is forever planning horrors for mankind and that by recognizing them as coming from Him, we can at least prevent them from being any worse. It pays God no compliment to assume that He is responsible for everything unpleasant that happens to us. Much of the unpleasantness we suffer is entirely our own fault, and allowing that much of it may come from the malice and stupidity of others, we do wrong to put all the blame on God. Later in this study we shall see how God *permits* evil while He *wills* good. We should guard against concentrating on what He permits to the exclusion of what He wills.

While it may be easier to see the will of God in what is painful than in what is pleasurable it is nevertheless true that God designs us more for happiness than for sadness. Sadness is a negation of happiness; it is not something that exists in its own right. Sadness may be very necessary to us, and in this sense it can be looked upon as a good, but it is not something to be aspired to and enjoyed as a positive possession. So it is strange that we should connect it with the will of God more often than we connect happiness with the will of God. "I suppose I have to accept this trial as God's will," we say with a sigh. Do we so readily shout with joyous recognition of God's will when something happens that pleases us? Gratitude gets just as near to the will of God as resignation.

It is important, then, to think of God's will as something positive, as a vital force with which we can become identified, and not merely as something restrictive and imposed in virtue of God's prerogative. In our recognition of God's will, it would be something of a waste to stop short at bowing to the inevitable. God's will should be an invitation, a challenge to the service of love. Once we grasp the truth that God wills man's happiness, we ought to be able to hail joy as the gift of God, as an incentive to recollection, as among the clearest indications of divine providence.

Another trap that lies open in the estimation of how God's will touches our affairs is the view we grow up with of God Himself. If we are honest with ourselves, do we not regard Him as one who maneuvers us into positions that suit His plan and from which we cannot escape except by His miraculous intervention? The misconception arises partly from the false idea of prayer that we learn as children, partly from the idiom of piety that looks more to the extraordinary than to the ordinary ways of grace, and partly from our quite understandable tendency to judge the mind of God by what we know of our own.

First, what are we told about prayer? We are given to understand that it will get us out of every difficulty. From our earliest infancy, the belief is drummed into us that if we repeat our petitions often enough, we shall get what we want. Faith and perseverance: armed with these two we cannot miss. Now, all this is perfectly true, but not in the sense that we normally understand it. Prayer *does* get us out of every difficulty — by so building up our inner reserves that we meet every difficulty and rise above it. If we repeat our petitions often enough, we *do* get what we want — because we come to want God's will even more than we want an answer to the particular petition we are making. Given faith and perseverance, we cannot miss — since in proportion as these qualities deepen, we get closer to our true goal, which is God.

Sometimes, it is true, the more obvious meaning of the doctrine is verified. We pray, and the obstacle vanishes. We place complete confidence in the power of God to work a miracle, and the miracle (to everyone's surprise, including our own) happens. We make up our minds never to give up asking, come what may, and after a while, we are rewarded with exactly what we have asked for. Instances of this sort are happily common: they strengthen our belief in the power of prayer and provide occasions for showing gratitude to God. The thing to remember is that such examples of cause and effect are not the only ones that prove the value of prayer, and that those which show it less clearly are evidence of greater faith, greater love, greater trust and generosity.

The next source of misunderstanding is the peculiar phraseology of popular devotion. Printed prayers, hymns, exhortations from the pulpit, little ferverinos that we read in letters from religious men and women: all seem to suggest that the ways of God belong to a quite different world from the one we know, and that if we are to tap the sources of the spirit, we must use a formula we would never dream of using in our dealings with people. It is true, of course, that the order of grace does not operate according to the laws of nature, but at the same time there must be an affinity between the two, or we would never begin to understand the order of grace at all.

Speaking about the way in which grace works, our Lord uses the illustration of seed growing to maturity in the field. The farmer sows, goes home and attends to other things, comes back at the proper time, sees how the development has been getting on, and eventually reaps. The implication here is that the dealings of God with man follow a more or less accepted course, and that only on special occasions do they deviate into the extraordinary. Yet if we went by the idiom of piety, we would be assuming a different manifestation altogether. We would look for God's will in the spectacular, await God's mercy in the dramatic, expect God's peace to reveal itself in placid contentment.

The trouble is that we have our own ideas about how God's will is to be revealed, and since these ideas are colored by self-interest, they are almost always wrong. Like Naaman the Syrian, we instinctively leap to the grandiose, picturing to ourselves a sensational cure of our particular leprosy, when in fact God operates in a commonplace setting and through materials without glamor.[21] The error is a not unusual one: James and John fell into it and were corrected by our Lord, who called them "sons of thunder."[22] If we turned more often to the Gospel for our cue as to how God's will operates, we would get nearer to the truth than by studying the candy-coated opinions of the devout.

A missionary prays for the grace of martyrdom. Fine. Ideally speaking, and all things being equal, there is nothing much higher that he could pray for. But what if it is emotionally and not ideally speaking? What if all things are not equal? And in fact, they never are. Grace infallibly comes in answer to the missionary's prayer, but it is not the grace expected. Perhaps he is sent home to the mother house to do the accounts or to answer the door. Not at all the martyrdom he wanted, not at all the heroism

[21]4 Kings 5:10-11 (RSV = 2 Kings 5:10-11).
[22]Luke 9:54-55; Mark 3:17.

he pictured to himself. But a grace nevertheless, and the will of God nevertheless.

Or take a less obvious example illustrating the same theme. A wife prays that her alcoholic husband be released from his slavery to drink. Nothing can possibly be wrong with that. For the husband, drink is an evil, and she is praying that he be no longer tempted. Grace, again, infallibly comes. But not necessarily in the form of a physical cure. The man does not suddenly find himself disgusted at the sight of a bottle. The smell of liquor does not put him off his food. What happens is that something happens inside his character; he is given a chance of seeing more clearly and acting more resolutely. He is perfectly free to act upon or reject the grace. The attraction to drink may remain as powerful as ever, but there is an added strength with which to meet it.

Now, say this man fails, and goes on drinking with undiminished purpose. Is the wife to assume that her prayer has been fruitless? Not at all. What she should do in this case is to see that no obstacles are put in the way of the ordinary course of her husband's cure. If she is driving the man to drink by nagging at him, she is counting too much on a miracle when she prays that he may give it up. It cannot be too much insisted that the grace of God, which is the same as the will of God, comes to us normally through normal channels. Grace builds upon nature; it does not jump over it unless, for some reason, God wills a miracle. The best preparation for supernatural intervention is the right use of the natural. Where ordinary means are provided, ordinary means should be employed. It is when ordinary means are not provided that we can start thinking about miracles. It is comforting to reflect that whether ordinary or extraordinary, all means directed by a right intention toward good come under the providence of God. God's will does not have to wait for the heavens to part before it declares itself.

∞

Now, for the third of our mistaken approaches to the subject — the tendency to read God's mind by comparison with our own. Experience of our mental processes shows us a directing organ that is highly variable. We change our minds every few minutes, we come under the influence of other minds, we are never absolutely sure what our mind on any given subject really is, we make up our minds on the spur of the moment to meet a particular situation, there are subjects about which we genuinely believe ourselves to have a completely open mind, and there are whole areas of life in relation to which we have no mind at all. (How often in the day do we say, "It doesn't interest me" and "I don't mind"?) God's mind does not work in this way.

God does not change. He is eternally the same. If God could change His mind, He would stop being God. God is never swayed by our prayers as we are swayed by the pleadings of fellow human beings.

Yet we talk as though the intensity of our faith were able to influence the mind of God. Our prayers cannot be stronger than God's decisions, or God would have to abdicate in favor of His creatures.

It is perhaps here, in this matter of the otherness of God's mind from ours, that the source of all our confusion lies. If we could grasp what is meant by the everlasting sameness of God, we would get a better idea of how His will operates in the world and in our own souls. We would understand how His mercy is always waiting for the sinner to repent, how His presence is always with us, how His love is the only reason there is any love in us at all, how impossible it would be to misplace whatever trust we put in Him.

Prayer and the Will of God

∞

Not only can God's mind never change, but His love cannot change either. We human beings possess a different kind of heart. Our hearts are as variable as our minds. But with God, His love is the same as His will — eternal and unchanging. Human beings love now one person, now another. Sometimes they love God, and then another love comes along and the love of God dies down. It is one of our sad human limitations that there is room in the heart for only a certain amount of love. Love in this life is incomplete; we are physically and emotionally incapable of loving everybody indiscriminately all the time.

But with God this is not the case. God does not change toward people as they change toward Him and toward one another. With Him there is no division or sequence of operation as regards love. And because His love and His will are one, His infinite and universal love must mean an infinite and universal will toward the good of man.

The implications of this touch us at every point in our lives, at every waking and sleeping moment. It means that loving us as He does, and in virtue of His infinite wisdom knowing exactly what is best for us, God never stops willing our highest happiness. In all that we do, God wants us to aspire to the perfect happiness that is His alone to give. Our Lord tells us to ask "that our joy may be full."[23] It is important that we appreciate the attitude of God toward His creatures, establishing firmly in our minds that His love and His will are one, because very often we follow our Lord's injunction to ask and are rewarded with no sort of joy at all. If God is forever willing our highest happiness, how is it we taste so

[23]Cf. John 16:24.

little of it? If God is almighty, can He not bring about our happiness more often — especially when we ask him in His Son's name to do so?

The answer to such misgivings is seen at once if again we compare God's way of loving with our way of loving, God's way of willing with our way of willing. In our case, there are division, opposition, starting and finishing. In God's case, everything is one, and there is no beginning or ending.

Take first our human way of acting where love and making decisions are involved, and then see how God's way is bound to be different. Say you have a mother who loves, devotedly but injudiciously, her son. The love may be lasting and self-sacrificing, but because it is human, it will be vulnerable. The son pleads, and the mother gives in. The mother may know in her heart that it is a mistake to give in, but her love is in opposition to her judgment. So in consenting to her son's demand, she is willing for him the lesser good.

In the case of God's love for us, the situation is quite different. His will cannot oppose His love because they are the same thing. He cannot "give in" to a mistaken course of action on the grounds that love excuses everything. Yet is not this what we imagine Him to be doing all the time, what we hope He will do next time we pray for something we want very much?

When we speak of God's "consenting" to our request, we should not think of an alteration taking place in the mind of God. It is not as though He had decided in the beginning upon a course of action in our regard, and then, because of the new light shed upon the matter by us in our prayer, is now prepared to fall in with our idea. All along He has willed what was most for our good; the only thing our prayer has done is to bring this will into play. Moreover, this prayer of ours, which has seemed to have had such telling effect, was not an invention of our own; it was inspired by

Him in the first place, or we could never have made it. On the occasions when our prayers are heard in the terms requested, what has happened is simply this: God, willing a certain effect to result upon the condition of our praying for it, has given us the light to see what was wanted and the grace to ask for it.

In view of what has just been said, it should not be difficult to understand how prayer is essentially a rising of the soul to meet the will of God. If we think of it as a drawing of God's will down from heaven so that it coincides with ours, we think of it mistakenly. Even the specific act of petition, so often insisted upon in the Gospel, is to be valued not for what it manages to get out of God, but for what it gets out of us. It cannot get out of God what God has not from all eternity wanted to give.

If we look again at the two illustrations given earlier, we can follow, now that the idea has been developed further, a wider application of the same principle. Thus, had the missionary and would-be martyr been granted his opportunity of laying down his life for Christ, he might not have made as good a job of it as in the providence of God he was granted to make of his bookkeeping and answering the door. The merit attached to any work is measured solely by its conformity to the will of God. God rewards only His own works, the works occasioned by His own will. Nobody understood this more clearly than St. Paul when he proclaimed that without the right motive for doing so, it was no use delivering one's body to be burned.[24] Without charity, St. Paul claimed, martyrdom was vain. And what is charity but the union of man's will with the will of God?

Love in this context is not the emotion but the conformity. If we unite our human will with the will of God, we have charity,

[24] 1 Cor. 13:3.

and we can do that whether we are called to the degree of charity that is crowned by martyrdom or to the less exciting degree that expresses itself in the commonplace. The one qualifying factor is the will of God.

The second illustration is more complex but the providential exercise of grace can be traced in the same way. The woman prays for her husband, and so far as outward results go, the prayer is fruitless. But who is she to judge? For all she knows, there may be a dozen good reasons, seen only by God, why her husband should be allowed to fail. His present weakness may prove the impulse to a penitence of heart that he never would have arrived at had he jogged along in a state of self-satisfied temperance. Without his repeated lapses, she herself might never have turned to God for help. Her trial of faith and hope, combined with his humiliation, may be giving great glory to God. Others, unknown to this struggling couple, may be receiving grace as the result of the suffering. God has a wider screen presented to Him than man has, and it is a mistake for us to question the often bewildering permissions of His will.

To conclude this section, and by way of commentary, it is worth quoting from a document found on the body of an unidentified Confederate soldier during the Civil War:

I asked God for strength that I might achieve; I was left weak that I might learn humbly to obey. I asked for power that I might lead, and win the praise of men; I was given weakness that I might feel the need for God. I asked for health that I might do greater things; I was given infirmity that I might do better things . . . I got nothing that I asked for, but everything that I hoped for. Almost despite myself my unspoken prayers were answered. I am among all men most richly blessed.

Whether or not he was a Catholic, whether or not he had any theology, the writer of those lines had learned what was meant by the phrase "the will of God." There is always an inwardness to the way in which God treats His creatures, and we are given the grace of faith precisely for the purpose of accepting that inwardness and acting upon it. There is an outward way by which our lives are conducted, but it does not carry us far enough. The external may be, indeed most often is, misleading. So with St. Paul "we look not at the things which are seen but at the things which are not seen; for the things which are seen are temporal, but the things which are not seen are eternal."[25] The will of God is in the things that are seen (or they would not even come to light in the first place) but to see it there is only half the battle — the easier half. The difficult part is seeing the will of God in the obscure, the frustrating, the apparently inconsistent and even contradictory. Difficult but not impossible: we are given the grace to trust.

[25] 2 Cor. 4:18

Chapter 9

∞

Responding to God's Will

One of the main conclusions to be drawn from what has been said so far is that God's will shows itself not as a ruling that comes from without, superimposed upon life as a religious extra, but rather as a force in life and through life. It is something the effects of which we see outwardly and acknowledge, but the reality of which is an abiding part of life itself. Indeed it *is* life itself, because without God's will, life would not only be meaningless but would be non-existent. "The wind cannot be seen," said Socrates, "but can be known by what it does," and just as the waves on the sea and the leaves on the tree bear witness to the activity of the unseen wind, so the circumstances of our lives and the events of history bear witness to the unceasing and underlying operation of God's will.

So if we are looking for God's will, and we come into this world for nothing else but to search out His will and fulfill it, we know where it is to be found. It is everywhere around us in the happenings of life; it is inside us, drawing our souls toward cooperation and union. Admittedly, we may often find ourselves completely in the dark as to which of two or more courses to follow is the one God wills us to choose, but this does not mean that God's will is not there for us to discover. God does not suspend His will, as if He were lifting the map out of our hands and telling us to get on with our journey unaccompanied by His grace, because if He did, we would cease to be. It is His will that "conserves" not only us human beings but the whole of creation. The universe (the cosmos and space and all the rest of it) hangs upon the will of God, hinges upon the will of God, proceeds in its pace and rhythm according to the will of God.

When all this has been said, it can be seen how some ideas are really too big for human language and that the will of God is one of them. To claim that creation "hangs" upon the will of God, "hinges" upon the will of God, is to suggest no more than that God supports the work of His hands as a pear tree supports its fruit and that He keeps the earth spinning around as the mechanism in a fairground keeps the painted wooden horses in musical circulation. But what the will of God does is far more than this. It gives being itself. Take away the will of God, and there is nothing. Not even space.

Allowing then that words and images are not much use, we still have to use words and images with which to form our ideas because they are the best we have got and they have been given us for this purpose. Perhaps we get closest to the idea of God's will animating His creation when we think of it as God breathing into the work He does, into the works we see and live with and are. It is the illustration He himself chooses when He begins to reveal Himself in holy scripture. He breathes life.

The act of breathing is something continuous — not something switched on to meet a particular emergency. It is something largely unnoticed yet absolutely vital. If beyond a certain point we get out of breath, we die. And there is this highly significant feature in the illustration: that for the lungs to breathe in, they must also breathe out. Neither inhaling air nor expelling it is the whole of respiration; life needs both exercises equally. The impulse comes from God; He breathes and gives life. But the impulse must be followed up: we breathe back.

If you look up the references to breathing in a concordance, you will find enough material for meditation on the will of God to last you a lifetime. Notice particularly how our Lord breathes into the dead body when He restores a life, how He breathes into the apostles when giving them their apostolic powers. Compare this with the priest breathing into the child at Baptism, the bishop when confirming and conferring orders. Life comes with the will of God, and the will of God comes with life. But the beauty of it is that we do not have to wait for the breathing of God's will; it is going on all the time and in every place. Our true happiness, our holiness, consists in breathing the breath of His will back to Him from whom it comes.

Seeing the matter from this angle may not greatly affect our set prayers, but it should widen our concept of the function of prayer. By it we should come to a better appreciation of God's unsleeping interest in our affairs, of the loving concern which is ours for the asking — indeed, which is there even if we fail to ask — and of the manner in which prayer cooperates with the work of God in the guidance of mankind.

Take an example. Say you are asked to pray that the light of the Holy Spirit may direct the deliberations of a particular assembly. Suppose it is a question of an election or the passing of some important measure. You recite the required prayers and await the result. What is it that you are really expecting to happen? Do you think of it as training, by means of a combined effort of prayer, a beam of light upon the issue to be voted on — and so securing a clear pronouncement of God's will? Or do you think of it as the development of the Holy Spirit's life in the assembly, in each member of the assembly and in the body as a whole, so that when a decision comes to be made, there will be a greater desire for God's will than there was before? Granted that you are ready to see God's will in the outcome anyway, you must surely be approaching the subject at a deeper level when considering it in the second of these two ways. The set form of the prayer may be the same either way you approach it, but to see the work of the Holy Spirit as an overall influence, as the will of God becoming clearer in the measure that the voters yield themselves to it, would seem to hold more promise of fulfillment than to see it as pinpointing the agenda sheet and spotlighting the voting space.

The fact once established that God's will is the source of all that is, there should be no great difficulty in linking up human affairs with their origin. This is effected by the virtue of religion. The word *religion* derives from the Latin *re-ligo:* "I bind back." Practicing religion we bind ourselves back to where we belong. We have been separated from God by sin, and religion puts us right again; we rejoin our proper element. In this true environment, everything speaks to us of God, everything represents God's will. The more we come to live our religion, the clearer we come to hear the voice of His revelation and the quicker we become in recognizing the representations of His will for what they really are.

A man is stricken with polio. It is the will of God, coming to Him independently of himself and from outside. But more significantly, the will of God is inside him, inviting his cooperation with the affliction. "You must accept it as God's will," his friends tell him. Yes, but it is going to make a big difference how he accepts it. Must he think of it as God's willing him to suffer? He can if he likes, but a more helpful emphasis is given to the trial if he thinks of God's willing away inside his soul and giving him the grace to meet his polio in its true terms.

A man loses the ignition key of his car and cannot start for work. He reminds himself that it must be the will of God. "God has planned from all eternity," he tells himself, "that I should lose the ignition key on this particular morning when I am in a hurry to get to the office." There is nothing theologically wrong with this, but the stress is on the wrong thing. Better to say, "God has willed from all eternity that I should rise to this sort of annoyance, and this is what I mean to do; my will inside myself is accordingly in line with His." And incidentally, it is the will of God that the friend whom he telephones, asking to be picked up, should apply the same principle. The wife who is searching behind the cushions, the small son who has swallowed the key and has to see a doctor, the grandmother who is in a state about the whole affair: all can benefit spiritually in the same way.

Or take a less obvious example when it is a question not of an outward happening that indicates the operation of God's will but of a decision to be reached. A girl wonders if she has a vocation to the religious life. She feels an attraction to the cloister, but the married life appeals to her too. Which does God will for her? Before we go any further in this, let it be said that God's will is not going to be debarred from her if she chooses wrong, if she chooses according to self instead of according to grace. But suppose she is bent on choosing right, on choosing God's will, whatever her own preference declares itself in the end to be. In the meantime, she prays about it and awaits a clearer indication. Now, surely in such cases of genuine doubt, the way to get light is really to want God's will and nothing else. It is to identify one's human will in anticipation with the eternal will of God, which, it may confidently be hoped, will emerge from the fog. So long as there exists a selfish prejudice either way, it is not in the interests of the soul to see the doubts resolved. Rather than declare His will before the soul is properly detached from self-seeking, God allows the genuine darkness to continue. Better to be in the dark about what to do next than to see what God wants and then to go in the opposite direction.

A ball is lying motionless on a table. Tip one side of the table or the other, and the ball rolls off. If the ball is to remain still, the surface on which it rests has to remain still. If, in making decisions that have for their object the glory of God, we incline one way or another toward self, the soul is not steady enough to receive the movement of the spirit. So, in the case of uncertainty regarding vocation, the way to get light would be to mean the clause in the Our Father that chooses God's will. God's will in one form or another is going to be done anyway, but what the soul here is looking for is the chance of serving God's will rather than making do with God's will.

One last illustration before moving on to further argument and theory: A teaching sister is told by her superior to take over a certain class. The sister dislikes the subject, dislikes the children, and dislikes the superior. But she goes ahead with it because she knows that it is the will of God for her to do so. It would be no more and no less the will of God for her if she liked the subject, liked the children, or liked the superior. But although her likes and dislikes do not affect the will of God so far as the outward act of obedience goes, they may well affect her own inward response to the will of God. It is again the question of breathing in and breathing out: the dual function of the will of God.

There may be more merit in the distasteful than in the agreeable, but merit is not the final qualification. The love of God is the final qualification, and love is measured, as we have seen, by the degree to which we unite our wills with the will of God. At our judgment, we shall not be asked whether we enjoyed doing the will of God but whether we did it. So long as we satisfy ourselves (and God) on the basic requirement of loving His will, which means doing it, we can safely leave the question of merit to be settled in the lobby.

"But in all these examples you have cited," it might be objected at this point, "the eventual outcome cannot but be the will of God. Win or lose, God's will is covered."

Of course. What we are trying to show here is that from *our* point of view, we gain far more by adapting ourselves inwardly to the call of grace and *choosing* God's will although we would far rather not. We have the chance not merely of making a virtue of necessity but of perfecting the virtue, whether the necessity is there or not.

The bride in the Canticle sought for the Beloved in the streets, but he had already passed through the streets and was found ultimately in her own soul.[26] The will of God is in the marketplace, the classroom, the hospital ward, the battlefield, the car-park, the cocktail party, the stadium, but unless it is recognized in the individual human soul, it is a doctrine merely, or at best a theological fact. Rightly understood, it can become a presence. It can be to the soul a reality compared with which all outward happenings and concrete things seem woefully insubstantial.

Ignoras te, pulcherrima — "you do not know yourself, O beautiful one." What the Bridegroom is saying is that, unaware of the

---

[26]Cf. Cant. 3:2.

indwelling reality which is hers and which is the quality that makes her beautiful, she has no idea of what she really is. Until she has realized God's will within her, she is not fully aware of what is going on. This is what St. Augustine means when he says, referring to the time before his conversion, "You, Lord, were within me, and I was without." Such a realization is not simply an acquired knack, a twist of fancy. It is a habit of grace to be cultivated by response to grace. It means industry as well as insight, but once the point of perception is reached, it makes a big difference to religion, spirituality, day-to-day prayer.

Seeing in every circumstance a pointer and a reminder, the soul becomes more or less habitually conscious of the operation of God's will. Surrounding circumstances help the interior activity, the interior activity evaluates the surrounding circumstances. Although for the teaching nun we have talked about earlier, there was her vow of obedience to accentuate her recognition of God's will in the work proposed, there is for everyone, vow or no vow, the same chance of recognizing God's will in whatever has to be done. The ordinary sequence of events, unavoidable for the most part and a lot of them indifferent either way so far as the emotions go, speaks to us of God's design, and comes to us therefore from the planning mind of God.

Although it is true that circumstances do not shape our destiny for us, do not inevitably mold our characters, it is also true that according to what we bring to them, the circumstances of our lives can be the means of either our sanctification or rejection. What we bring to them is either recognition of God's providence or rebellion against it. If we do not get in first and shape them, applying the doctrine of the will of God, there is always the danger that circumstances, applying the pressures of a materialistic world, may shape us.

Responding to God's Will

∞

More than two centuries ago, a British ship was sailing far out at sea off the coast of South America. The expected rains had failed, the inhabitants of Brazil were hostile, and because the supply of drinking water on board had run out, the men were dying of thirst. Desperate in their necessity, they signaled to a passing ship (the account of the incident does not say whether it was Spanish or Portuguese) for enough fresh water to help them out until the rains came. To their dismay, the signal came back to the British seamen instructing them to lower their buckets over the side and take as much as they wanted.

Was it a joke? The message went out again, in still more urgent terms, and the reply came back to the effect that since they were surrounded by water, the British should try using it. Eventually it was decided to let down an experimental bucket, which, when drawn up on deck, was discovered to contain not salt but fresh water. What the British did not know, but what was common knowledge to those who sailed those seas, was that the force of the Amazon was so powerful as to carry its waters miles beyond its mouth, rendering the seawater harmless.

On all sides we are surrounded by an element that supports us; it is the element by which we are appointed to travel. It does not seem to afford us what we want. We look elsewhere. In our thirst for the things of God, we look up at the heavens, and when no moisture comes from that quarter, we complain that the heavens have dried up. We turn to the coastline, and despair of help from there. We send out signals of distress to others who are on the same sort of voyage as we are. When we are told what to do, we think we are being made fools of. Eventually, because we have tried everything else without success, we follow our instructions and find that the solution has been there all along.

75

Prayer and the Will of God

∞

It is significant in this connection that in the *Rituale* of the Church are printed official blessings for every sort of commonplace object. The implication here is that linen, bread, bells, rooms, clothes, tools and farm implements, typewriters, and handcarts can become the material means by which the soul reaches out to supernatural good. In themselves, they are just inanimate creatures to which nobody pays much attention until they are needed for a particular purpose, but in the scheme of God's will, they are playing a part as vehicles both of the divine purpose to man and the human response to God. It is as if the Creator is bent upon so saturating His creation with Himself that creatures may assist one another in the recognition of His activity.

If this should suggest a danger of pantheism (the heresy that identifies God with the universe), there is ample corrective in the thought that creatures, taken in the wrong way, can do just the reverse. The truth is that while material things are far from being split-off pieces of the divine essence, as some have argued, the whole of life is so penetrated inside and out with the supernatural that wherever we turn, we cannot evade God's will. Remember the psalmist's rueful acknowledgment:

Lord, You have known me sitting and standing; You have seen into my thoughts from afar. My course You have searched out, and all my ways You have foreseen . . . whither shall I go from Your spirit, whither *flee* from Your face? If I mount into the heavens, You are there; if I go down into the deep, You are there too. How early soever I take wing, hiding in the utter remoteness of the sea, it will be Your hand that leads me, Your hand that holds me up. I told myself that perhaps darkness would cloak me about, that night would be on my side in my pleasures. But again darkness is not dark to You; the night is as daylight to Your gaze. Wherever You look, it is the same to You . . . for to You there can be nothing hid.[27]

Indeed, if we turned more often to the psalmist for enlightenment, we would enter more deeply into the mystery of God's will than by consulting psychiatrists and cataloging our motivations. "In the head of the book it is written of me," he says in the thirty-ninth psalm,[28] "that I should do Your will. O my God, I have desired it, and to have Your law in the midst of my heart." Notice how this bears out what we have been considering: the inward response of the human will to the outward demand of the law — and the relation between the two constituting God's will. Again and again in the psalms we get this idea of obedience to the design, the frame, the lines, the dispensations, the testimonies and justifications of God. God's word is everywhere about us; we cannot escape His truth.

St. Augustine says that God's will is our "firmament," but even this, unless it is taken to mean the air we breathe, does not get us close enough to the reality. God's will is a more intimate fact than the firmament of the sky, the canopy under which all our acts are performed. God's will is the impulse of our acts, the motor power without which we could not do a thing or understand His word. It is by God's will, to quote the psalmist again, that we are "established in His sight forever" and can say, "Blessed be the Lord from eternity to eternity. So be it." This *fiat, fiat* with which the

[27]Cf. Ps. 138:2, 4, 7-12, 15 (RSV = Ps. 139:2, 4, 7-12, 15).
[28]RSV = Ps. 40.

fortieth psalm closes can be taken to sum up all that has been said so far. Indeed, if we truly mean it, our *fiat, fiat* can stand for the whole of our religious service. Practiced in its perfection it defines sanctity itself.

Chapter 10

∞

How the Saints Fulfill God's Will

This is the place to examine the way in which the challenge of God's will is met by those who must be the chief exponents of the principle. In a later chapter, we shall consider how our Lord fulfilled the Father's will, but for the moment, our investigation takes us to those ordinary human beings like ourselves who are perfectly free to follow their own will if they want to, but who in fact have chosen to follow the will of God.

For such, the opening verses of St. Paul's twelfth chapter to the Romans may be representative: "I beseech you therefore, brethren, by the mercy of God that you present your bodies a living sacrifice, holy, pleasing unto God, your reasonable service. And be not conformed to this world, but be reformed in the newness of your mind, that you may prove what is the good, the acceptable, and the perfect will of God." The contrasting wills are shown here: the will of the world and the will of God. The soul must choose. The service of God is "reasonable" — more reasonable actually than service of the world — and if the will of God is to be proved in its fullness, there has to be an interior reformation. Forswearing conformity with the standards of the world, the truly religious soul is urged to go about the service of God in "newness of mind." While the body is presented as a living sacrifice, the mind is presented in the same terms — as sacrificial material. There is here the same relation that we have noted before between the outward and the inward. In the adjustment of the one to the other lies the fulfillment of the perfect will of God. Man's whole being, flesh and spirit, is the area of transformation. If one or the other, human sense or human mind, is left out, the balance is disturbed and the potential perfection is disqualified.

In case the objection is raised here that this is hardly material for beginners, it must be insisted that as a matter of fact it is. You cannot even begin unless you know what is expected of you. A saint is only a beginner who has gone deeper into the truths with which he began. There is not one law for beginners and one for experts, one spirituality for beginners and one for mystics, one will of God for beginners and another for those who are finishing. Holiness is simply the degree to which the human will is united in love to the divine, and unless we start off intending to unite our wills with God's, we can never advance at all. It is a mistake to think of what the saint does in the way of service as something different in kind from what we do; the difference lies in the amount of love he puts into it. The will of God is for all of us the same — our sanctification. How far we achieve this end will depend upon the joint forces of God's grace and our response. "Be you therefore perfect"[29] is addressed to all.

The proposition arrived at, then, is that we undertake some sort of reformation of heart and mind in order more perfectly to serve God rather than the world. This change is known by the Greek word *metanoia*, and by it we judge the affairs of life in a new way.

[29]Matt. 5:48.

They are the old affairs of life, but they are seen in new perspective. The deeper understanding of God's will ensures this. In the alchemy of grace, the many facets of God's will are no longer seen in diversity but in unity. As the beginner develops in his purpose, he sees more and more what God's creatures represent. At the start, he could acknowledge the presence of God's will only at intervals and in major events. He would read of a war breaking out somewhere, and would say to himself, "I suppose that must be in a curious way God's will"; someone would die, and he would be forced to bow to God's will. Even for that amount of recognition, there has to be a certain groundwork of *metanoia*, or he would accept the purely materialist assumption that these things were of terrestrial significance only and could be accounted for without reference to a divine plan.

But then, as the beginner goes to work on his *metanoia*, he is brought up sharply and often by what can only be evidences of God's will. Gradually, grace working within him, the beginner looks at the world around him as a setting for the performance of God's will. He sees history as the movement of God's will. He sees sorrow, and even more mysteriously, he sees sin, as part of the pattern of God's will. Where before he judged that a lot must be happening which God can scarcely have allowed for, now he can look this side of life in the face and know that nothing is going on behind God's back. He does not have to make excuses for God: he believes in the existence of a design. He may not see how things fit in, but he knows without question that they must.

So it can be appreciated that God's will is becoming comprehensive where hitherto it was piecemeal. It was comprehensive all along, but the beginner did not see it so. God's will is becoming identified with God's love. They were the same thing all along, but the beginner assigned to them respective operations. "I know what is meant by the love of God," he had said, "because from it flow tenderness, mercy, and answers to my cry for help." Would he have been so clear about the will of God, or would he have thought about it as something else again? Certainly if we may go by what the saints say of themselves, we see a great simplicity resulting from their labors. The testimony seems universal. Whether he happens to be apostolic or mystical, intellectual or peasant, leading churchman or obscure layman, the saint is everywhere found to be a man of one idea: God's will.

Man comes to his knowledge by means of evidence from outside, by experience and practice. He does not learn all at once, but part at a time. This is true of a trade, of a skill, or of a science. People sometimes imagine that their understanding of a subject is immediate or congenital, that their talents express themselves perfectly by instinct. This is asking a lot, and short of an infused grace, the abilities we possess may be claimed to have developed gradually. Even in the case of the sacraments, where the grace *is* infused, the exercise of the appropriate virtue is a matter of progressing step by step. The facility is reached, but not automatically.

Before he can get a broken-down car into running order, a garage mechanic has to have picked up his knowledge from bits of metal. He has learned that certain combinations of bolts and screws and wires produce certain effects. Car maintenance is no longer a problem; he can drive without thinking. But it was not always so.

Or take a musician. The composer may have a gift to start with — he must have, if he is to be any good — but he learns from notes and instruments. He gets into the way of arranging isolated spots on a piece of paper so that they make up a musical score. He can finger bits of ivory, wood, metal, and strings with such sureness that the required noise results. But before this can happen, there have to be observation, intake, and correlation. A translation has to take place inside if anything is to be expressed outwardly.

A better example than either of these would be the way in which a doctor comes to treat the living human body from what he has learned as a medical student from the skeleton. The study of an object composed of many separate bones kept together by wire and hanging from a hook has given him his knowledge of anatomy. The living organism gives him far more to work on in his practice, and he is picking up new knowledge every day, but as a beginner, he had to start with the bare bones, the frame.

The point is that only when the beginner has reached the stage of dealing immediately and experimentally with his material does the knowledge that he has acquired become part of him. The same is the case of the beginner with the will of God. "This is the will of God, your sanctification,"[30] and without man's will to sanctify himself, God's will remains unfulfilled. God's will may be halfheartedly acknowledged, intermittently obeyed, but unless it evokes the kind of response that the human will is capable of rendering — "your sanctification" being possible by God's grace — there is something missing.

God's will is therefore a summons. It is as though God were saying, "Give yourself to my will, and I promise to do the rest." From recognition, through acceptance, to identification. This is the classic sequence, the perfect service.

For the will of God to come into its own as a living, vitalizing entity, not stopping short at the letter of the law, there have to be souls in the world who are dedicated to it. Such souls we call saints.

[30] 1 Thess. 4:3.

∞

So, when you get right down to it, what would be the attitude of mind you would expect to find in a saint? Must it not be something that would express itself in some such form as this: "I pledge myself wholly to the will of God, confident that whatever my obedience to its demand involves, I shall not be left without the help to comply with it"? Self-surrender and trust: because these assume love, they assume everything else.

In the Old Testament, the verbs *to sacrifice* and *to sanctify* are used to mean almost the same thing. So, when we come to the New Testament and read our Lord's prayer to the Father which contains the statement, "for them do I sanctify myself, that they also may be sanctified in truth,"[31] we know at once, even if we did not know what was to come in the Passion, that there is here the added implication of sacrifice. Our Lord is saying more than, "I am schooling myself to a high level of conduct so that my disciples may know how to behave"; he is saying, "because I have surrendered myself to Your will, *they* must." What Christ wills for Himself, He wills also for His disciples. "My sacrifice, with their own sacrifices united to mine, must define the nature of Christian perfection. If they are looking for Christian holiness, they must know its conditions. If they are to be sanctified in truth, they must sacrifice their wills in truth. This is what I have willed for them because it is what You, Father, have willed for me. I can pay them no higher compliment than that."

It can be judged from the terms of the commitment that not all who claim to be Christians would claim to go quite so far. Small blame to them. Truth is to be preferred to humbug. One has to

---

[31] John 17:19.

84

begin somewhere. The question each individual has to ask himself
is not, "Am I completely and irrevocably dedicated to the will of
God at its highest and most taxing level?" because the answer, if
honestly given, is pretty well bound to be discouraging, but rather,
"Am I trying to let the will of God mean more to me?" If we can
rise to the challenge of this second question, we are not doing too
badly; we have at least made a start. There is about the attitude at
least something of a dedication. Perhaps it is only the finished
product in sanctity who can answer the earlier question without
blinking.

To be sanctified in truth really means *truth*. No self-deception,
no hiding behind grand talk, no vaporizing about a will of God
that, when examined, turns out to be only one's own will with a
holy label. The dedication may not be the total burnt-offering
that one would like it to be, but at least it must be true as far as it
goes. Confessed limitations are more pleasing to God than untrue
pretensions. The practical problem becomes this: how far up the
scale can the human will be pushed so that it more nearly approxi-
mates God's will for its perfection?

For an answer, we can look to the tenth chapter of Hebrews,
where the process is outlined for us thus: the law is provided by
God as both the frame of our human operation and an earnest of
things to come; but the law does not of itself and automatically
make us perfect; something else has to be added if our service is
not to stop short at exact observance; *mere* ritual purification does
no more than dispose the soul; a positive reality has to be intro-
duced, something (or better still, someone) capable of wiping out
guilt and sin and evil generally, and exercising the supremely qualifying influence for good, has to come along and the human will
has somehow (which means, of course, by grace) to identify itself
with that force, with that Person, with that will.

Then, by way of confirmation, the letter to the Hebrews quotes the thirty-ninth psalm. "Sacrifice and oblation You did not ask for, but a body You have given me. Holocausts for sin were not enough for You. So I cried: 'Behold I come.' The very first thing that is written of me in the book is that I should do Your will, O God . . . then I said: 'Behold, I come to do Your will, O God.'" When Christ comes into our lives, He comes in His completeness — with His will perfectly united with the will of the Father. And when we try to come closer to Christ, we come with our wills, choosing, for all our imperfection, to unite our wills with His.

It can be readily understood what an expanding influence such an attitude must exercise. The idea is completely mistaken which makes the religious man egocentric. The truly religious man is concerned about everything except himself. Having committed himself to God in perfect trust, he does not bother to sort himself out as he used to do. He knows that he will get farther in God's service by trust and love than by self-analysis. If there have been saints who were introspective, it is not because their pursuit of holiness made them so, but because they were introspective to begin with, and even their holiness did not cure them of it.

So when St. Augustine defined *sanctity* as "to live by God for the sake of God alone," he was not narrowing the saint's horizon but, on the contrary, widening it. God's interests, which are wide enough to include the whole of His creation, are now the soul's interests. God's will, which desires the good of every single individual in the world, is reflected in the saint's attitude of wishing well to all mankind. Nor is this just a vague, all-embracing benevolence such as a naturally friendly man would feel toward his fellows, not just a warm glow such as most of us would admit to on occasions like Christmas, but rather, it is the kind of charity that stands up to the test of personal self-sacrifice. The saint, because

God did so in the person of Christ, goes out of his way to help and to save. He expects good to come out of sinful human beings, and where sin comes out instead, he is prepared to forgive. He works toward the perfect manifestation of God's will, and where he sees rebellion against God's will, he is not dismayed. He knows that divine love is stronger than human malice.

Indeed, one of the mistakes the would-be saint has to guard against is that of allowing himself to get too much upset by the evil in the world. He has to see sin and go on hating it, but he must learn to take its existence in his stride.

It is related of St. Francis that in the beginning of his conversion, the distress he felt at the thought of God's love being rejected, of the innocent being corrupted, of wickedness flourishing even among those who should have been shepherding Christ's flock, was so great as to hinder him in the work he had undertaken. He expended more energy in weeping over the frailties of man than in trying to correct them. But as he advanced in holiness, he came to a better balance in this matter, detaching himself from his over-tender feelings and making allowance for what God's will evidently allowed for.

So it would seem that if we are to do the work of God as apostles of His will, we must avoid getting — to use the apt American phrase — "emotionally involved." (The English, with their quaint terminology, would murmur something about not letting the windscreen-wiper run away with one.) The true apostle is confident that God has not abandoned man, and that grace will triumph in the end. To focus all attention upon vice might lead to despair; to call for the exercise of virtue is to echo the voice of God's will.

The apostle is a workman like any other. True, his work is full of the grace of God, but while his feet are still on the ground, he remains a realist. He can have as many ideals as he likes, the more the better, but he must go about the service of God with his sensibilities well under control. People often imagine that their love of God is outraged by the evidence of men's sins, when really it is not their love of God that is hurt so much as their nerves. Nerves, the product of a passion, must be mortified if God's work is to be done effectively. What would we think of a craftsman or laborer who allowed his emotions to dominate his job? Would we employ a decorator a second time who, having painted and cleaned up the house, came back a month later in floods of tears because he had heard we had messed up one of the walls? In the armed forces, which are rightly called "services," a display of natural sentiment would be even more out of place. In the service of God, which is the highest employment of man, natural sentiment must give place to supernatural purpose. This means will.

The service of God — and particularly, of its very nature, the service expressed in the apostolate — involves close personal relationships. How can we not become committed? How can we remain detached? The problem is a real one, never altogether finding a satisfactory solution. But once again, the answer must lie not in the deeper understanding of our own mixed motives, whose whole business it is to yield unreliable findings, but in the deeper understanding of God's will. If we truly intend to find, pursue, and perfect God's will for us in the relationships that entangle us, we shall eventually come to view them within the pattern of His providence. It is only when we trust to luck that we are left to luck. Those things that we hide from God, God hides from us. Our safety lies, once more, in the realist approach: we face the issue as it is in God's sight and ask that we may come to see it as He sees it.

Furthermore, it must be remembered that God does not show us things as He sees them unless at the same time He gives us the grace to handle them as He wills them to be handled. What would

be the point of our seeing either the danger or the solution if there
was nothing we could do about it?

A certain saint (whose name I unfortunately forget) trained
himself to repeat over and over again, hundreds of times a day, the
clause from the Our Father "Thy will be done." This practice he
regarded not as a devotion but as a necessity, for whenever he left
off, he was assailed by the most urgent temptations against faith,
chastity, and hope. As time went by, he found himself reduced to a
state of extreme nervous tension, rattling off ever faster and faster
"Thy will be done," until he began to realize that there was an essential connection between the content of his prayer and the un-
suspected nature of his temptation. Could it not be said that the
Father's will *was* being done when temptation assaulted his soul?

On the showing of St. James's letter, this would seem to be the
case. "Count it all joy when you fall into diverse temptations,
knowing that the trying of your faith works patience . . . blessed is
the man who endures temptation, for when he has been proved,
he will receive the crown of life which God has promised to them
that love him."[32] Even if he could not go so far as to count it all joy
when the attacks were raging, he could at least acknowledge the
permissive and providential will of God. For an investigation of
this aspect of God's will, we shall need a separate chapter. It is a
pity I cannot recall the identity of the saint referred to; he would
surely come in useful to many. Anyway, he bears out in his experience the point we have been trying to make in this chapter.

[32]James 1:2-3, 12.

Chapter 11

∞

Discovering God's Will in Our Lives

The merest glance at the history of heresies will show that it is the will of God in one form or another that the heretics have got wrong. In the early Church, there was the question of reconciling the divine and human will in the person of Christ. Later it was the difficulty of seeing how the wisdom of God, which is His will just as it is His love, operated in a Church that was composed of human beings. In Reformation times, the Protestant theologians of Germany, Switzerland, and France, developing a much older heresy, held that God willed some to be saved and others to be damned and there was nothing one could do about it. Later still there were the Quietists of the early eighteenth century who taught that to attain to sanctity, Christians must abandon themselves so totally to the will of God as to eliminate altogether the action of their own wills.

This is not the place for either a history lesson or a theological exposition, but if the reader is to get any sort of idea as to the relationship between God in heaven promulgating His eternal will and man on earth apparently twisting it out of all recognition, some mention must be made of the theologian's distinction between God's antecedent and his permissive will.

Prayer and the Will of God

What beginner has not wondered at the seeming discrepancy between the doctrine of an all-wise God whose guidance is forever drawing the human race toward full stature in His divine Son and the factual indications to hand? Can wisdom itself choose unwise means to attain the required end? In going over the argument, it should be borne in mind that the term "mystery of God's will" is a valid one. We are never going to arrive at a completely satisfactory understanding of it; but at least it will be something if we come to see the part played by human cooperation with it. Since the ground has been covered before in this series, the briefest survey will suffice here.

Working back to God from what we know of ourselves, we can trace an antecedent and a permissive way of willing in our relationships with one another. We desire, obviously, for our friends the best that life can bring. Antecedently we are willing them full happiness. While it is true that, as fellow human beings, we have no power to bestow this happiness upon them or make conditions for its realization, we possess at least this much in common with God: we leave the world wide open to make its own destiny. In other words, we exercise a permissive will toward those whose happiness concerns us. We feel responsible *to* them, because they are objects of our love, but not responsible *for* them, because they enjoy their own inalienable freedom.

The parallel is lamentably inexact, but bring it to bear on the infinite love which God has for man. Antecedently He wills nothing but good. In His love and wisdom, He has given to man as His greatest gift the power to accept or reject His will. The liberty of the human will is that which more than anything else makes the human soul resemble the divine. So, although God positively wills one thing in the created order, He allows in that created order which has known the Fall a different thing to happen. Had there

92

been no Original Sin, the distinction would not have been necessary: man's will would have obeyed the will of God, would have chosen to fall in with God's designs all along the line, and there would have been no evil consequences to call for God's permission. But with the rejection of willing service, man's action is fraught with unhappy result. The so-called problem of evil is not explained away by this aspect of our first parents' failure but merely made less of a mystery.

For most people, the difficulty is not so much with the existence of pain and suffering in a fallen world as with what actually happens when the will of God for a particular person is one thing and the person decides to do something else. Must this not in some way devalue God's will, making it depend upon a perhaps purely frivolous decision of man?

Again an example may serve. Assume that a devout and rich man feels urged to build a church. He decides, after praying about it, that God wills a church to stand in a certain area. Many Masses will be offered, Catholics will be able to get to the sacraments who would otherwise be deprived, conversions will follow, and a new center of the apostolate will be established. If this rich man were to die or lose all his money, there would be no great problem. Anyone who knew about the project would assume quite naturally that it was the will of God: a pity, but manifestly the will of God.

Say, however, the rich man stays alive and stays rich but decides to open a racing stable instead. What has happened to the will of God? There it was, all ready, and a mere man has reduced it to nothing. Death and financial loss can be regarded as acts of God, and justified accordingly, but here was an act of man. The principle remains the same in each case: the actual outcome is what God has willed, and this is far more certain than that He ever willed a church to be built in the first place. Short of a direct revelation on the subject, it would not be for anyone to claim a knowledge of God's antecedent will in the matter.

A point that remains open is what has happened in the mind of the rich man. Is his will now in line with the will of God? The answer must depend upon how far the undertaking had represented to him a real demand: how sincerely he had originally believed that a church was required of him. His change of plan may be anywhere between a serious rejection of grace, tantamount to turning down a clear vocation to the religious life, and a lighthearted deviation from what had been no more than a temporary religious enthusiasm. But whichever it is, and wherever he stands between these extremes, the grace is there now to help him make the best of the circumstances as they have turned out.

This is an important thing to remember, because often it is felt that once we have neglected to cooperate with God's grace at a high level, we are disqualified from cooperating again. Such a view would suggest a vindictive, even a touchy God. "All right: you have failed me over something which I wanted; now I shall cheerfully fail you over the things that you want. You have refused the heights; you can get along on the plains by yourself."

St. Teresa[33] at one stage lacked the generosity to accept the grace of contemplation. But by making use of the graces measured to her lower state, she eventually got back to where she had been before, and higher. It took her twelve years, and although to the end of her life she was full of remorse for her early infidelity, she was glad enough to have paid the price of getting back. Her experience teaches a twofold lesson: it does not pay to turn down God's offers, but if we do, we have other offers waiting for us lower down the scale.

---

[33] St. Teresa of Avila (1515-1582), Spanish Carmelite nun and mystic.

To be balanced against all this, the beginner, or even the seasoned practitioner for that matter, does not have to take every noble impulse that comes to him as being the will of God. Only scruples and confusion would result. The noble impulse has to be valued in relation to surrounding circumstances. There have been instances in the lives of holy people which suggest that the interior attraction to a certain course is both so strong and so clear as to override all secondary considerations, but such occasions must be looked upon as the exception. In the ordinary way, the urge, particularly if it calls for heroic or histrionic expression, must be looked at in the cold, hard light of reason, against the dusty, flat backdrop of actuality.

A young married couple decide that the most unselfish thing they can do is to have a mother-in-law as a permanent guest in their house. "This is a good thing in itself, and we feel the same about it," they argue, "so it must be the will of God." But must it — just like that? God will certainly bless their generosity if they follow through with the scheme, but it is equally certain that before doing so, they weigh it up according to prudence. How will it affect their marriage? Will it mean that the children's education will have to suffer? Will friends no longer come? Will arguments or example give scandal? Admittedly, the main issue is the one to pray about, but these side issues may not be brushed aside as unworthy. They would not be there if they were not worthy, so God presumably wills them to act as guiding lines.

Where circumstances point in a particular direction, and still more so, of course, where they force a particular situation, the recognition of God's will is relatively easy. But often we have to search for God's will in a tangle of alternatives.

Our liberty of will is a great gift, but sometimes we wish we did not have so much of it. If only God, or even someone else acting in

His name, would decide for us. Our job is to *discover* (in the strict sense of uncovering, and so bringing to light what is already there) God's will in the exercise of our freedom, not to *produce* it by sleight of hand from an opinionated self.

Even in the religious life, where obedience might be thought to take care of everything, it is only too possible to make the will of God seem anything but what it is. The deluded religious can maneuver, fooling himself and other people. It is also true that however pure his motives, the religious can be as much at the mercy of his mistaken judgment as can the layman. Is he to accept, for instance, a position of authority that is offered him but not imposed? Say he genuinely believes himself to be unequal to it. Is he wasting a chance of furthering God's work for souls by playing safe, or is he taking the reasonable means of averting disaster? Ought he to make the supreme act of trust in God's grace and go ahead, or does God want him to use his freedom of will to back out while the backing is good? Neither circumstances nor the opinions of others tell him everything. His own judgment and his own experience may yield no information. What is he to do? There is nothing else he can do but pray. If he prays with a detached heart, it does not matter which alternative he chooses. If he really wants only the will of God, he cannot miss it. Indeed, if he really prays, he has got it already, before he makes the choice.

Accordingly if we are sincere when we say in the Our Father, "hallowed be Thy name," we are pronouncing an earnest of the next clause, "Thy kingdom come." An earnest also of the one after, "Thy will be done on earth as it is in heaven." These three prayer acts, whether regarded as acts of praise or petition, are not entirely eschatological in their implication. They can be applied to the immediate and temporal just as they can be applied to the general and eternal. "Hallowed be Thy name" in the Chinese rendering of the Our Father becomes "may all men do homage to Thy name as holy." By looking toward a time when living people universally worship, the soul is both assuming the power of God and begging the power of God to bring it about.

There is nothing humanistic about this regard for the perfection of mankind on earth; the concern is that all men may unite with the activity of grace, and so give perfect worship to God. Back once more to the breathing in and breathing out. Granted that God's spirit informs the human soul, the human soul can breathe the prayer of the blessed in heaven and mean all that "hallowed be Thy name" implies.

∞

Another facet to the subject, and one that has margins of contact with those considered above, is the Quietist misconception mentioned already. Without adopting a heretical position, people can take the view that if God's will is always present in their lives, doing its perfect work anyway, the best thing is to let it run on without any help from them. The direction here is straight toward fatalism.

As propounded originally by the circle of mystics and recollects, the tenets of Quietism looked innocent enough. Indeed, they looked highly spiritual and sanctifying. The human will must be so wholly surrendered to God's will that it desires nothing, hopes for nothing, and does nothing except under the direct action of grace. Nothing much wrong with that. But in fact it was heading for supine inertia. "God's will" became a fetish; man's will became a cipher. Orthodoxy would have been preserved had a measure of human cooperation been demanded, but cooperation was held to be quite enough in the way of operation to spoil the work of God. The soul was required not to transform self but to annihilate self. Prayer for the Quietist was not just a matter of keeping the emotions still so as to simplify the act of the will; it was a matter of eliminating activity of any sort, whether of the emotions or of the will.

Madame Guyon was to write of the soul perfected by grace that "it is as little possible for it to distinguish itself from God as God distinguishes Himself from it." On such a showing, the human individual, when made holy, has no longer any real existence of his own. He is not an entity working for the fulfillment of God's will; he is not even a passive instrument wanting to be used; he is a vacuum, an emptiness. If God cannot distinguish Himself from such a soul, He is clearly not the God of Christian teaching. At least the Quietist errors had this effect: they showed us the necessity of using our wills *as* wills. The highest thing a human will can do is freely to will God's will.

If this means anything at all, it means that there must be occasions in life when it is not enough to sit back and wait for God's will to roll over one. There are times when, for the very fulfillment of God's will, the initiative has to be taken. In the event, the action may prove to have been misplaced or untimely, but this is not to say that it ought never to have been taken. "It is God's will," says Bossuet, "that we should do nothing listlessly," and one of the dangers of too much abandonment is that we come to do everything listlessly. How not — if we feel guilty about doing anything at all?

Any school of spirituality that jettisons the moral autonomy of man, even if it is in the name of giving greater glory to God, is bound to fall foul of Catholic teaching. For us, the way of giving glory to God is by being ourselves — by willing and acting in harmony with the vocation God has given us. Such action is free and individual. If we so sacrificed our liberty to choose God's will, we would be machines and would give only a mechanical glory to God. If we so sacrificed our individuality as to become merged in a kind of general human fluid, where would be the doctrine of a personal redemption?

Although the theology of Quietism is dead, the Quietist way of thinking is very much alive. More alive now, since the arrival upon our horizon of nuclear weapons of destruction, than twenty or thirty years ago. People imagine it to be a virtue to wait upon the will of God long after the will of God has been suggested to them. There is no merit in passivity as such. "*Do* unto others," our Lord says, "as you would have them do unto you."[34] He speaks about positive undertakings more often than about getting out of the stream of life. Talents must be traded with, wheat must be sown and harvested, leaven must spread. "I have finished the work," He was able to say at the end, "Thou gavest me to *do*."[35] "Indeed, this was the Son of God,"[36] could be said of Him when He had finished; "He did all things well."[37]

We have to do more than merely accept the evil in the world; we have to resist it. Yet to judge from a trend in present-day spiritual writing, stagnation is better than sticking one's neck out. Are we never to initiate, but always to allow other people's initiations to dominate? Are we never to reform, but always to assume that God's will is directed against change? Are we never to correct offenders on the grounds that offenses are the due expressions, in a fallen world, of God's permissive will?

Put in these terms, the way of passive endurance may look ridiculous, but there is not a very clear line of demarcation between the passive endurance which is of God and that which is sheer sloth. It would be sad if we of this period in history, of all periods, evaded our responsibilities because of a muddle-headed understanding of

[34]Cf. Luke 6:31.
[35]John 17:4.
[36]Cf. Mark 15:39.
[37]Cf. Mark 7:37.

the will of God. More will be said about this in the concluding chapter.

If the doctrine of conformity to God's will is to mean invariable acceptance of the existing order, then it would be imperfection ever to change anything at all. A soul would do wrong to change from the lay state in order to enter religious life; a single person would have to stay single because such was the state to which he happened to belong. But God's will not only allows for changes but often demands them. It is likely to demand a number of significant changes as the result of the Second Vatican Council, which itself would never have been convened were the *status quo* to be infallibly identified with God's will.

It is perhaps typical of our age that people enjoy the hunt more than they enjoy the find. It is a commonplace to observe how useless is the pursuit of leisure if people do not know what to do with their leisure when they have got it. It would seem to be the same with regard to the will of God: people talk a lot about it, and are forever harping upon how assiduous they are in the search for it, yet when the will of God is shown them, they look the other way. Important as search and expectation are, they are not to be rated above performance.

A few months ago, I was sitting in a doctor's waiting-room in Bristol. Also waiting were two other men, neither of whom I knew. One was reading back issues of *Country Life*; the other, too agitated to read, was restlessly moving about and looking at his watch. After a while, this second man came over to where I was sitting, and said this: "Everyone gets ill at some time or another. I've been ill before, and I've known it was all part of the day's work. But this time, it's the wrong illness." Then, since I had no comment to make, he added, "And it's come at the wrong time." The other man, without looking up from his *Country Life* and showing no sign that he had heard, said, "But to the right person."

If we believe in the providence of God, it is always the right person who gets the right expression of God's will. If there is mystery in much connected with the subject, there is nothing but straightforwardness here. However straightforward the principle, even however blatantly obvious the manifestation, there is always the obstacle of what might be called escapeful thinking. When presented with the occasion, we look for a way around it, for a way out. Our view of God's will is bifocal: long-sightedly we see it coming, near-sightedly we fail to recognize it.

It is a curious thing that while we in America and England are more free than most with our counsels of perfection, we are noticeably reluctant to follow them to their conclusions. Historians may well point to this era as one in which the religious idea was matter for popular discussion. But if all this inquiry does not have the will of God as its aim, it might just as well not be going on. People will tell you airily they are searching for truth, and if you talk to them about God's will, they object that you are being too narrow. If they are looking for a truth that is "broader" or "more objective" or "more scientific" than "religious" truth, it is not surprising that they miss truth itself when they come across it. The truth of God is the will of God, as it is also the love and the power of God, and unless it is sought on its own terms, it is mistaken in the substitutes men have made for it. The will of God may contain a mystery, but there is all the difference in the world between a mystery and a confusion.

Chapter 12

∞

Embracing God's Will

The response of the human will is easily tested. It is simply a question of whether we make, to the point of acting on it, the divine will our own or whether the words "Thy will be done" are no more than a presumed passport.

You may object that even this fails as a touchstone because it is by no means clear what is meant by "making God's will one's own." All right, by way of explanation we can once again draw upon the relationship between two people who are fond of one another.

When a husband or wife says, "Leave my wishes out of this: you should know by now that in marrying you, I made your happiness more important than my own," we have a reasonably clear idea of what is implied. Such a remark must, if it is sincere, come from a heart that is not greedy for its own satisfaction. There has been self-giving here; there has been recognition not merely of another's rights as a married person but of something else that, although obviously suggested by the marriage vow, is not explicitly demanded in the contract. The handing over has been complete. "Whatever makes you happy, that I choose. As far as I am concerned, alternatives no longer present themselves: I follow a single course — the one that pleases you."

In man's relationship with God, the situation is much the same. By implication, the Christian is committed to what pious books used to call the "good-pleasure" of God. The graces of Baptism are such that they destine the soul that makes proper use of them to the highest holiness and to the fulfillment of God's good-pleasure. The Christian obligation admits of a minimal service, but it calls to a maximal one. Just as a married person, by satisfying his responsibilities and not being unfaithful, is honoring the requirements of marriage, so the Christian, by trying to keep out of mortal sin, is fulfilling the letter of the law. Such a Christian is obeying the will of God, but he can hardly be said to have made God's will his own. He is not putting God's *good-pleasure* first.

To "make God's will one's own" is accordingly to establish a single criterion. It is to forget about rights and personal inclinations; it is to look only to one guiding principle. On the negative side, it is to discount prejudice, worldly standards of judgment, and material advantage; on the positive side, it is to make love the final arbiter. When the human will has surrendered to the divine will as fully as this, then God's purpose in creating the soul has been achieved and life for that soul assumes balance and order; until such a surrender has taken place, balance and order are uncertain. (This point will be developed in a later chapter, when the effects of conformity to God's will are examined.)

When St. Paul urges the Corinthians to "do all their works in charity"[38] this is exactly what he means. If they love the will of God more than they love their own wills, they must inevitably be doing works of charity all day long. They will be willing what is

[38]Cf. 1 Cor. 16:14.

best; they will be loving God and their neighbor in the ordinary things they have to do. And the things that are done to them, whether bringing joy or sorrow, will be received in charity. Having chosen God's will in everything, they see everything as evidence of God's will.

In the eighty-third psalm,[39] the sacred writer expresses this interaction between the human and the divine will. "My heart and body have rejoiced in the living God . . . Blessed is the man whose help is from You, O God, for in his heart he has purposed to mount by the degrees appointed . . . The lawgiver shall bestow his blessing, and they shall go from virtue to virtue . . . Better is one day in God's house above thousands. I have chosen to be abject in the house of my God, rather than to dwell in the tents of sinners." The soul has made the choice of God's will in preference to temporal pleasure, so it can rejoice in being abject if abjection is the state God bestows. God is the lawgiver, and whatever comes from the lawgiver, be it pleasing or painful, is a blessing. Those thus blessed go, inevitably, from virtue to virtue; God's help, which is His will, goes with them.

The serious choice of God's interests in preference to self-interest involves a considerable reorientation. It means that self's whole interest is pleasing God. Self is pushed out of the picture. Nor can self, still looking around for satisfaction as it will go on doing without willing to, claim any great merit for what seems so heroic a choice. Self recognizes the full truth of our Lord's words: "You have not chosen me, but I have first chosen you."[40] In the practical order, the change of focus is found to make a great difference. It means that instead of serving God in the way we think He ought to

[39]RSV = Ps. 84.
[40]John 15:16.

like, we serve Him in any way we can — which will be the way He wants. We let God choose the way. Instead of putting our confidence in various practices of prayer, penance, charity, and so on that we have devised for ourselves, we shall be putting our confidence in His handling of our lives. What we would draw up in the way of a scheme or rule of life may objectively look far more "perfect" than what in fact is required of us by God's will. But "perfection" now denotes only one thing: God's will. When the soul has surrendered to all that is God's will, there is no longer any need to bother about different interpretations of perfection.

A would-be saint cannot always be certain that extra fasting is going to please God, but he can always be certain that self-surrender will. Hours spent in prayer *may* be a form of self-indulgence; surrender to God's will can never be. It is the substitution of the whole for the parts; it is directing attention to the end instead of to the means. The service of God is not to be restricted to performance; it looks to the attitude of mind and heart. Outward execution follows the inward actuation; it is no substitute for the activity of the will. When a man's will is united with the will of God, the acts he performs flow from a more significant source than ingenuity in devising a form of service.

People, and especially beginners in the spiritual life, so often mistake the theoretical and idealized will of God for the actual. A girl, for instance, will judge that the most perfect thing for her to do is to leave the world and become a nun. In the counsels of perfection, there is every justification for this: "If thou wilt be perfect," our Lord said, "sell what thou hast, give to the poor, and follow me."[41] But the point is it may not be the vocation for *her*. She has been right to judge that she is called to perfection, but

[41]Cf. Matt. 19:21.

mistaken in judging that the convent life was to be the setting for it.

She makes a trial of the life and after a period of trial comes away. The test of her essential vocation is still going on, and is perhaps more searching now than when she entered the novitiate: What is her attitude now toward the will of God? Much will depend upon whether she looks back with resentment or with gratitude; whether she looks forward trusting to luck or believing in God's providence. She can say either, "The whole thing was a delusion. I was a fool to aim at perfection. I gave myself to God, and He has shown that He does not want me. In future I make no offers, thank you, and will follow my own will," or, as she is being given the grace to say, "I went in because I thought it was the will of God: I can assume, therefore, that although He did not mean me to persevere He did mean me to try: I came out because it was God's will that I should: all I have to do now is to find out what kind of perfection He wants from me, and where I can best realize it; what I want above all is His satisfaction; my happiness is His will, and His glory is my will."

It may be inferred that in the more strictly interior order of prayer, the same principle will apply; there will be either confusion and discouragement, followed perhaps by the decision to give up praying altogether, or there will be abandonment in faith to the purpose of God. In the beginning, there may have been all sorts of preconceived ideas as to how prayer ought to be made, as to what it would feel like when going properly, as to the stages that might be expected in the advance toward the higher mystical transformations. Then, in the actual experience of prayer, comes something quite different. The question is now, as it was in the case of the girl who had a vocation to try her vocation but whose true vocation was to something she had not thought of, which way will the soul jump? Is it to be: "I should never have started on the course of prayer. It was not for me. If I want to serve God, I must find some other way. This experience has been a stumbling-block to my faith"? Or is it to be: "I have no ideas about prayer anymore. I am incapable of practicing the methods suggested. I want to praise God in my prayer, but I find I cannot do it. I do not know the meaning of love; all I know is that if God wills this state for me, a state that seems a waste, I will it too. His will means more to me than my spiritual satisfaction or sense of security; His will is my whole desire"? If the ultimate test is looked for, this is it.

In case some may see in this doctrine of substituting God's will for one's own an alienation of something that we have no right to alienate, it would be as well to clear up the point before taking on anything else. The whole weight of the argument rests on the fact that man only really begins to live when he has begun to die to self. Far from being contemptuous of human freedom, the theory sees true human freedom as being realized only when the human will surrenders itself wholly to the divine. So it is not so much an abdication as an initiation. There is here no loss to human personality but rather infinite enrichment.

The reason most people are unsure of themselves is because they have never properly found themselves in the context of God's will. If all men made it their first objective to discover God's will and live by it, they would find for themselves not only the individualities God meant them to have and develop but also help to create the environment God meant them to have and develop. God's will would then be standard throughout the world — standard not in the sense of a force compelling regimentation, but in the sense of grace and truth inviting cooperation. It is only because man's final purposes and immediate endeavors become so overshadowed by what *He wants* that they drift farther and farther away from the providential scheme. The wider the gap, the more difficult it is for the individual human being to see the relationship.

Hence the many confusions in the world. If the connection between God's will and man's true interest were seen, how could there be any problem about civil rights, nuclear warheads, or aid to starving peoples? But since the connection is not seen, the remedies applied are at best social and humanitarian. Man is made in the image and likeness of God, and when this fact is overlooked, everything takes on a humanist character. So of course there is chaos. Where the source of human justice is left out of account, and the justice of God is His love, the human aptitude for injustice has only human uprightness to oppose it. In a fallen human race, the natural virtues, left to themselves and divorced from supernatural grace, are not enough.

So, for humanity at large, as for its individual members, the main trouble is that of not finding its destined place in the plan of God. Since we are here concerned more with the particular than with the general, we must get back to the soul's search for its true identity. This is a personal thing, a unique adventure in every case, so it will be more by prayer than by argument and study that any progress toward truth-in-self and self-in-truth will be made. What follows is given rather as an incitement to pray than in proof of a thesis.

༺෴༻

"A man must live his own life." This statement may be made by way of excuse, authorization, correction, or sympathy. It is not on any showing a very original reflection. But however superficial, there is an inwardness to the pronouncement that deserves a closer look. A man *has* to live his own life and nobody else's. A man has to *live*, and not merely put in time until he dies. A man has to come to terms with the life he is given, however dull or disagreeable the setting, whatever his aspirations to a nobler life, wherever the direction of his main interests.

In *The Shoes of the Fisherman*, Mr. Morris West makes one of the characters, a journalist, say, "I'm not a man; I'm just a name in a suit. There's no me at all. One push, and I fall apart." You meet that man every day; he is all over the world. You cannot even push him because there is nothing to push. There is no resistance to pressure. It is easier to help a strong character who is wrong than a weak one who is right.

Why are there so many — why are, perhaps, we ourselves — like Mr. West's fictional character (although it should be added that the character in the novel shows himself to be of tougher quality than his self-appraisal suggests)? Is it not because, in order to be yourself, you have to be the person God means you to be, and if you are not that person, you are nothing?

There is every justification for the present-day cult of the unhero; it is the attempted justification of ourselves. If we refuse to unite ourselves with the will that has created us for a specific purpose, we are rudderless creatures. Clinging to our own cherished images of ourselves, we sacrifice substance. If we surrendered ourselves to the true image that God has of us, frankly accepting the discrepancy between the reality of God's will and the dream we have created for ourselves, we would be not only holier and happier but also more of a help to other people. When what they want to lean on is something solid, how can people be helped by what is itself leaning on unreality? There can be no support but in truth, and there is no truth apart from God's will. We find our identity only in God.

It is a characteristic of the young to indulge in hero worship. Nature has arranged that they should. If the small boy of six did not admire his father and try to imitate him, there would be something wrong either with the small boy or with the father. At a later stage in growing up, during the period of adolescence and perhaps for a while after it, admiration and imitation go out to those with whom there may be no personal relationship and who may even be complete strangers. All this is a part of education.

Standards are not always conveyed by means of the spoken or written word, nor do they always come from the constituted authority. The impact may be made through example, appearance, mannerism, a particular ideal which is felt to be important. All this is perfectly normal, but if it is to be productive of good, there are two conditions to be satisfied: the hero must possess qualities that are worth admiring; and the admirer must retain his own personality. If the one admired is shallow, the influence is not likely to last; if he has character but no principles, the influence will be malign; if he has character and principles, and at the same time does not want to absorb the other's individuality, the influence is almost bound to be good — *almost,* because the other person's attitude must be taken into account. However admirable the hero is, and this would be true even if the hero is a saint, the admirer is a person in his own right and may not become a carbon-copy — even of a saint. Moreover, if he, the admirer, continues to model himself on someone else when he is no longer in the formative stage of normal development, he will remain forever immature. He will not be the integrated person God means him to be. He will belong neither to God nor to himself. He will be just a shadow.

In order to reach maturity, then, it is important not to get lost in someone else's maturity. True maturity is being oneself as a child of God. Many religious people make this mistake of taking up some saint and trying to mold themselves to the shape. But what if the shape is not the one God has designed? No two shapes are alike. All souls are made for God, but each goes by a unique way. Each has to decide whether to surrender to something less than God — and so becoming, if not a slavish imitation, a diminished person — or to surrender to the will of wisdom itself and finding identity and freedom.

Take the case of an ordinary humble man who does not know what to do with his life, who lacks confidence, who sees his contemporaries getting ahead of him, and who judges that his own lack of success must be traced to want of personality. He is no longer a boy; there is no hero to whom he can attach himself. So he follows one project after another, stirring up enthusiasm for each, but never seems to find himself in any of them. He remains, to draw from the jargon of the moment, self-consciously "unfulfilled." Anyone can see he is unfulfilled. True, it may be in the design of God that to go through life like this in fact fulfills the divine purpose, and that our man with the missing personality is discovering a secret personality known only to God. If this is so, it can only be because the will of God has been accepted, and that in drifting from one thing to another, the misfit has deliberately fitted himself into the providential design. (And this of itself would show that personality is present in abundance.)

Normally, however, a man is meant to find his vocation and himself in the life that declares itself. The vocation to be a misfit must be a rare one. Those who are restless and dissatisfied, ever questing and wanting to better themselves, are mostly too preoccupied with themselves to think about the will of God and the vocation to follow it in full perfection. Theirs are haphazard lives with scarcely any Godward direction. Projecting themselves into one role after another, they finally project themselves into the role of failure.

There is nothing wrong with failure when it comes as a grace from God, but it is not something to be opted for and dramatized. A false identification with God's will, whether by assuming it must always be what one wants it to be or by expecting it always to be calamitous, leads only to unreality. What is real in a man's character, and consequently, what is real in his experience, can come to light only insofar as it is related to the truth — to reality itself as it exists in God. Without God in his life, man is submerged. He lies under an ocean of self and sin and uncertainty, always trying to see the sky but unable to because of the waters that come between. There is only one way of rising to the surface, and then the sun does the rest.

All this is not an attempt to provide a simple, cellophane-wrapped remedy for nervous, psychological, and emotional disorders. It has a more positive purpose. It is intended to encourage souls to make the supreme act of trust. It is not to claim in romantic terms that, having done so, they will then be "launched upon the grand adventure of their lives" and that from now on they will have nothing to do but observe the smooth and beautiful wisdom with which God handles their affairs; rather, it is to claim that in the blood, tears, and confusion of life, there will be something to cling onto that nothing can possibly disturb. The psalmist knows all about this when, having just complained of the darkness in himself, he prays in Psalm 142[42]: "Teach me to do Your will, for You are my God. Your own good spirit shall lead me into the right land; it is You who brings my soul out from trouble."

[42]RSV = Ps. 143.

Chapter 13

∞

The Benefits of Accepting God's Will

Having cautioned against expecting a panacea, we can now examine some of the consequences that should in fact follow the commitment to God's will. The first and most noticeable result of entrusting ourselves to the good-pleasure of God must surely be a sense of security and relief. In pledging ourselves to divine wisdom, we no longer fear the outcome of our decisions, no longer doubt the value of our trials, no longer have misgivings on the score of wasted effort. We come to know beyond all question that we know nothing about our lives and that God knows all. This being so, it is with absolute confidence that we hand over the whole direction of affairs to Him.

Does this smack of fatalism, abrogation of personal responsibility, or smug detachment? No, not so long as we go on willing and so long as we go on working as though everything depended on our effort. There is a vast difference between "I needn't bother anymore; I've made the supreme act" and "I've made the act, and to prove it, I'll go on trying just as hard; but what happens as a result is not my business." It is the difference between sacrificing freedom and sanctifying freedom — a distinction that may not have been appreciated in the Old Testament use of the almost synonymous words *sacrifice* and *sanctify* but which is amply accounted for in the tradition of the New.

Freed at last from laocoönizing itself in a tangle of mixed motives, the soul that has surrendered to *whatever* God wills can meet the serpents one by one. No matter what God asks, no matter how complicated life becomes, no matter where our inclinations lie, no matter the degree of utter exhaustion to which we have been reduced, all we need to be clear about is that God's will is somehow coming through. This is the one thing that assumes any importance. The scale of values has now altered, and there is no longer room for — in the strict sense — disappointment. Incongruity is ruled out because an exact balance, according to this world's estimate, is not expected. Everything, even injustice and the suffering of the innocent, is assumed to have a reason. The ordinary stumbling-blocks to faith are stumbling-blocks no more, but rather mounting-blocks.

Accordingly, the anxieties that are common to most of us tend to lessen. We now stand in the words of the *Benedictus:* "to serve Him without fear, in holiness and equity,"[43] because those things which threaten our happiness must be powerless against a happiness that consists in willing the happiness of God.

An unhappy man is nearly always one who lives under the shadow of some dread. The present opportunity of enjoying life is darkened because he is all the time steeling himself to meet a horror in store. He is afraid he may have to go into hospital or retire from his job; he fears the death of someone he loves; he fears financial loss, atomic war, old age, death. Perhaps the fear is more subtle, and what he is afraid of is happiness or love. Or perhaps he

[43]Cf. Luke 1:74-75.

fears the sheer continuance of his unhappiness — whether he knows the cause of it or not.

Well, all this is at least made bearable, although possibly not much more than that, when underlying it is seen to be the will of God. It is made more positively worthwhile when embraced as the will of God and offered to the greater glory of God. Even failure in marriage, failure in vocation and aspiration, failure in being able to adjust to existing conditions — all the countless failures that normally engender fears and are engendered by fears — can be resolved in the context of God's love. "Perfect love casts out fear,"[44] but even a love that is imperfect goes a long way.

Man is not required to see the end, temporarily speaking, to which his experiences are leading him. Far better that it should be hidden from him. He can guess if he likes, but he will nearly always be wrong. If, however, he makes as the end of all he experiences a realization beyond human existence, then he acts sensibly; then he acts in faith. The sort of happiness he is now envisaging "neither the rust nor the moth can consume" and it lies beyond the reach of robbers who might steal it away from him.[45] Man can never entirely rid himself of fears, anxieties, and depressions because his emotions have to be taken into account, and these will go on disturbing him however well ordered the rational side of him has become.

Emotional disturbances can be the lot even of the saints. Sanctity is not proof against mind-body pressures. Instinctive reflexes, compulsions, chain-reactions: these things go on bothering people far advanced in holiness. The difference is that where holy people make allowance for them and keep them in their place, we

[44]Cf. 1 John 4:18.
[45]Cf. Matt. 6:20.

do not. We let them get on top of us. We let them escape from the frame of God's will and so assume new menace. It might be thought, for example, that to be habitually in a state of grace would ensure a state of contentment. "If I keep out of the occasions of sin, surely I am entitled to peace of mind." You are not *entitled* to anything, and your mistake lies in equating the spiritual with the emotional.

It is true that spiritual, moral, and emotional problems react on one another. But they still remain problems after the main problem, union of the will with the will of God, has been resolved. And they remain separate. If a person of spiritual aspirations decides upon a course of moral lapses, he will experience conflict. This is obvious. But even when he has got his conduct under control again, and is willing what God wills, his emotions may well tend to run off and give him cause for anxiety and upset. Although on rational and spiritual grounds he has no call to worry, nervously and emotionally he may feel himself being torn apart. We shall have occasion to return to this point when considering the mind of Christ under pressures similar to our own.

Viewing the subject positively, from the standpoint of what help true spirituality can bring, we can judge that objectively material remedies can take on a spiritual character when accepted as the will of God. Whether a man is suffering from mental or physical ills, he can make use of the natural curative forces in full confidence that they are a means ordained by God. If God's will traces the pattern of a man's life, then it can be taken to have provided the natural as well as the supernatural equipment for the ordering of that life. Grace, particularly the grace that comes through the sacraments, performs its therapeutic work upon the soul. If mind and body have their appropriate therapies, the discoveries of medical science still owe their origin to God. Most of us tend to dwell too much upon the fact that God afflicts us with diseases and not enough upon the fact that He also sends remedies to relieve them. If one lot represents God's will, so does the other.

But whatever we say about God's will and health, our main concern here is with God's will and happiness. Whether you call it happiness or peace of mind, you come to know the quality at a more significant level by union with its source than by anything else. Assuming that your religious objective is not the elimination of anxiety, nor even ridding yourself of temptation, you may stake your security on surrendering everything to the unqualified will of God. You lose your life in order to find it, and if you do not put your reliance upon the truth of this paradox, there is no knowing where else you can put it. Nothing carries such gilt-edge guarantees.

∞

A further consequence of abandonment to the will of God is detachment. This is not quite the same as what we have been discussing above, peace of mind, but it arrives at the same thing in the end. Someone who is centered on God is — and to that extent — de-centered from self. People can become so fascinated by the complexities of their lives, the multiplicity of their desires, the permutations of their daydreams, that they come to miss the one thing that really matters. God's will is the unifying factor in life, the universal denominator that brings simplicity, and when people try to bypass it, they must necessarily find themselves encumbered with every sort of complication. A holy indifference to self's ceaseless clamor for what is either of secondary importance or of no importance at all is one of the first signs that a soul has made everything over to God.

Those who belong to the world naturally want to accumulate as much of what the world has to offer as they can lay their hands on. Those who are dedicated to a science, an art, an ideology in such a way as to exclude interest in other fields are going to end up, unless they are careful, with an obsession. Those who make even of religion such an exclusive and intensive pursuit that they will override social and natural demands can become victims of delusion and religious mania. Unfortunately, we can make an obsession of almost anything. *Almost* anything. It is difficult to see how the will of God can become an obsession, but if it can, it must only be because the doctrine has been misunderstood.

Rightly understood, the doctrine detaches from obsessions, extravagances, and failures of right emphasis. Once someone has allowed himself the luxury of a mania, he has placed himself at the mercy not only of sane circumstance (which is always likely to interfere with his eccentricities) but also of attacks that his own mind has exaggerated. To entertain an obsession is, by definition, to put things in false perspective. The over-valuation of a part spells impoverishment to the whole. At first, other parts get neglected, and ultimately the whole balance is lost.

What this is leading up to is that God's will lies in the whole of a thing just as it lies in its parts, and to give the undue emphasis of an obsessive attention to one or another of the parts is a selective act that cannot be said to conform with God's will. It is a denial of the wholeness of God's will. It is an expression of self and not of service. *And* it is doomed to disappointment.

Obsessions are doomed to disappointment for this reason: although they are chosen very often by the will, they reside mostly in the imagination. The imaginary is highly vulnerable. Whether you let yourself become obsessed by health, food, money, sleep, time, silence, speed, sex, clothes, religious observance, or any of the hundred preoccupations that draw the mind to a pinhead point of focus, you let yourself at the same time become a prey to the imaginary persecution, the imaginary neglect, the imaginary criticism, envy, ridicule, suspicion, and the rest. You no longer see things in proportion. You cannot, because you do not see them as God sees them. In order to see them as God sees them, you have to detach yourself from your obsessions and attach yourself to the will of God. Once you *have* attached yourself to the will of God, you see at least enough of truth to make your exaggerations look childish.

We are not talking now about the perfectly legitimate concern that a parent should feel for the morals of the young, that a religious superior should feel for the spirit and observance of the community, that a missionary should feel for the spread of the Faith. Concern of this sort goes with responsibility and is healthy. Its absence would point to lack of either feeling or zeal, or both. But because there is here no obsession, there is also no panic. When the parent, superior, or missionary finds he is being stampeded into panic, it is time for him to question himself on his attitude toward the will of God. Although serenity does not always prove the possession of the supernatural point of view — because the godless, too, can be serene — panic cannot but betray a want of trust.

Take the panic, for instance, occasioned by scruples. Scruples come from a false conscience. What happens is that the imagination fastens on some aspect of sin, and exaggerates it out of all proportion to reality. Sin comes to be seen everywhere; the soul is obsessed with it. The soul is not looking for God's will, but for justification of its own groundless anxiety. It is looking so restlessly for relief that the will of God is not clearly seen. Since scruples are founded upon a process of reasoning that is invalid, they can be stilled only when the soul has submitted to truth. Once the human will has accepted as valid the reasoning that is imposed by obedience, in the place of that imposed by the imagination and a false conscience, the panic ceases. Why? Because the soul has accepted the will of God.

If obedience is difficult for the scrupulous person, and common sense useless to him for the time being, the virtue of trust is the way back to sanity. Trust in God's providence and in His mercy will lead to trust in the representatives of His will. Without the exercise of this confidence, expressed in submission to another's judgment, the trial of scruples can bring a soul to the verge of desperation. Often it is easier to bow to God's will in a disaster such as a death than in the word of an authority. God is not tied to a particular mode of communication, and for those who are blinded either by the shock of loss or by a conflict of opinion in a matter of obedience, there is always just enough light to see what is wanted. We know what He wants. He wants our surrender.

Here is a theme if anyone wants to write a fairy-story or a ballet. The scene is a lost-property office (I believe that it is called in America a lost-and-found department) and the time shortly before midnight on Christmas Eve. Every sort of object is lying about, the more portable on shelves and the unwieldy in heaps and against the wall. Umbrellas, bicycles, suitcases, birdcages, parcels, hats, wheel-barrows, rocking chairs, toys, pieces of Greek statuary, baskets of decaying fruit and vegetables. As the clock over the entrance strikes twelve, the doors open and every object flies out on its way back to its owner.

To us, there is the element of mystery and fantasy because we have no idea to whom the objects belong, and we are kept guessing as to how they are finding their way home. God, looking down from heaven upon such an assortment, knows exactly to whom each object belongs, when it came into their possession, when and where it got lost, and what journey would be involved in the flight to restoration. To us, all these things are unrelated to one another;

therein lies their surrealist charm. But to God, there is a pattern, and every single pair of glasses, every old deflated football, every china vase has its own special associations and its own place in the general scheme. There is nothing incongruous in a telescope lying next to a frying-pan — not more incongruous than a lion lying next to a lamb or the leopard next to the kid. There is intimate harmony between all these separate things, and God sees them unified in the unity of His will.

If the picture seems fanciful and farfetched, it at least illustrates what should happen when the human will tries to unite itself with the divine will and to see life from God's point of view. The mind comes to see unity in diversity, comes to experience the real meaning of simplicity. You get the idea in the canticle *Benedicite* from the prophecy of Daniel and in the *Laudate* psalms. All the separate works of God's creation — sea, mountains, rivers, animals, people, angels — come together in the single act of worship and submission to God's will. However scattered it looks, everything in the world fits in. Everyone with his own private, personal history merges with the history of mankind, with the history of God's providence.

Nothing, moreover — to return to the fairytale theme — is in the strictest sense "lost." If it goes astray, it can always be found again. It can be restored to where it belongs. The American term is perhaps better here: the office represents the lost *and* found. There is a place for everything, even for the stray. Even those who are not in a state of grace and who have no intention of saving their souls are, although in a somewhat oblique way, fulfilling the will of God. God has not had that purpose in mind — that they should rebel against Him — but the fact that they have used their freedom to choose, even though they have chosen wrong, is witness to His will.

In one of the sapiential books, we read of God's wisdom as "reaching from end to end mightily and ordering all things with gentleness."[46] Nothing is so mightily commanded that liberty gives way to compulsion; nothing is so gently arranged that evil is condoned by divine softness. God is always ready to forgive, but He does not take an easygoing view of sin. Nor is anything left to chance. There is a destination reserved for every created thing. It is odd that, although we are reminded about this by our Lord when He talks about the very hairs on the head being numbered, the blades of grass and the lilies having their separately appointed place in God's mind, and not even a bird's death going unnoticed,[47] we still think in terms of mass-production. Consequently, we think that it cannot greatly matter to God what goes on in *my* brain, which is only one of countless million others. It matters so much that He surrounds us day and night with evidences of His will, each of them designed to recall us to the unique providence He is exercising in our regard. On His side, nothing is lacking for the perfect fulfilment of His plan. On our side, all that is lacking is perfect cooperation.

The graces resulting from this will-to-will service could be numbered, subdivided, graded, and pigeonholed almost indefinitely. Indeed, every virtue must have God's will as its reason for existing in the first place — let alone for its perfect exercise. So rather than overcharge this aspect of the subject, we can conclude with a look at the effect of surrender upon the most important of them all.

[46]Cf. Wisd. 8:1.
[47]Cf. Luke 12:6-7, 27-28.

With regard to charity in relation to God, thought of simply as worship, identification with the divine will assumes both the desire to give glory and the actual execution. Whether the prayer that the individual soul feels it to be God's will that he should practice is vocal or mental, distracted or clear, private or public, the principle holds good equally: the intention is to serve God's will. If the intention looks more to the individual's will than God's, then the charity in the prayer is to that extent lessened. It is clear that those who take the precept in its fullest sense and seriously set themselves to love the Lord their God with their whole heart, mind, and soul have already envisaged God's will and admitted it into their lives. Just as in God, His will and His love are one, so in us, the response to His will is the measure of our love.

Turning now to the other aspect of charity, love of neighbor, we can apply our earlier conclusions about the unity and simplicity of God's purpose. The theme of the *Benedicite* and *Laudate* of the Old Testament is repeated for us, and in the warmer terms of human relationship, in the New. From our Lord Himself we get the symbols of the vine, the flock, the field, and the net — each one showing the work of the unit within the whole; each one illustrating the corporate nature of sanctification. In the letters, we have St. Paul teaching the same doctrine: different members of the one body working together for the life of the whole; a diversity of gifts but the same spirit; a breaking down of barriers between Jew and gentile, bond and free, Greek and Roman. All are one in Christ.[48]

Every time we recite the Creed, we acknowledge the unity and catholicity of our Faith. Charity is implied; simplicity is implied. But does the Creed lead on to logical performance? It

[48]Cf. 1 Cor. 12: 4 ff.

should. Assuming that we see God's will to be working in the unity and catholicity of the Church, we should not find it too difficult to rise to the next step. Unless we do — unless we base our love of neighbor upon the love and will of God — we shall be selective in our charity to others. Seeing the relationship between every human being and his neighbor, seeing also the human family in relation to God's will, we both deepen the quality and extend the scope of our charity.

Instead of driving a wedge between the twofold expressions of charity, the Christian who is himself integrated expresses charity in simplicity. He does not have to be told by a theologian that charity is undivided; he knows it. Books and sermons may be needed to tell him how to apply his charity, but his experience of God's will is all that is needed to tell him of its immanence.

Chapter 14

∞

Christ Our Model

As though to make perfectly sure that the human souls whom He
had made in His own image would not miss it, God revealed His
will in the form of a living person, divine and human at the same
time: His Son. At the Incarnation, the Word of God, which is the
same as the will of God, took flesh; our Lord is the will of God per-
sonified. So He is at once infinite love, truth, beauty, wisdom, and
perfection. He is also the way by which we go to the Father, and
the life by which we live. Incorporated into His life at Baptism, we
are members of His Body and sharers of His spirit. For the guiding
of our mortal affairs, He is our model or exemplar. Shaping our
lives according to His example and teaching, we have absolute as-
surance that we are fulfilling the will of God. The questions for us
Christians are accordingly: how are His standards to be seen in a
world that has greatly changed since His time, and how are they to
be valued and applied even when they are seen?

Thinking of our Lord simply as setting the pattern of our faith,
and leaving until later an examination of some of the things He
said, we have even before His birth a clear enough hint as to the
line to be followed in the understanding of His Father's will.

Prophecy had foretold the Father's will regarding the Messiah: He was to be born in Bethlehem, His mother was to be a virgin, He was to be a light to the gentiles as well as a savior of His own people. (There were other prophecies as well, relating to His Passion and death, but for the time being, we shall consider only the circumstances surrounding His birth.)

Notice how the providential will of God came to be fulfilled. Mary lived at Nazareth, so on the face of it, there was little chance that Bethlehem would in fact be the place of Christ's birth. Mary was a virgin, but since she was espoused to Joseph, it might have been thought unlikely that she would become the virgin-mother of the Messiah. Nevertheless, God's will was moving, and unconscious agents were carrying it out. In Rome, a census of the empire was decreed by Caesar Augustus. On the other side of Palestine, somewhere far to the east, scholars were drawing certain conclusions from their studies. In Bethlehem, wives were becoming pregnant and giving birth. As a consequence of these apparently unrelated happenings, and in spite of what might have been expected, God's providential designs were exactly realized. Joseph, belonging to David's line, was required to register at Bethlehem, which was David's city. Mary, having consented to her vocation as delivered by Gabriel, fulfilled her role of virgin and mother. The first embassy of the gentiles, in the persons of the wise men, recognized our Lord both as King of the Jews and the light of truth for which they had been looking. The Holy Innocents were there to cover with their martyrdom the flight into Egypt.

When people complain of the haphazard nature of their lives, they should think of the apparently haphazard nature of our Lord's life, and then consider the marshaling of events, motives, and other apparently haphazard factors. It is not only in our Lord's life that everything was set for the fulfillment of the Father's will. In our own lives, too, everything is set and ready for our maximum cooperation. We are none of us in the lost-property office by accident. There is no such thing as, in the accepted sense, coincidence. Would you say it was coincidence that when Domitian sentenced to death those who claimed royal descent, he did not include those of David's line whose poverty and obscurity ruled them out as potential pretenders, and that Joseph's insignificance as a carpenter was because his branch of the family happened to be down on its luck? Would you say it was a coincidence that somebody in Jerusalem happened to have owned a donkey that had never been used to the yoke and that a request for just such a donkey was made to him at a particular moment during the week before the Pasch? That it was a coincidence to meet a man carrying a pitcher on his head and who happened to have a room to let when these facts had been announced beforehand? That a certain rich man had happened to have a tomb ready, and not before occupied, when our Lord's body was taken down from the Cross?

So the two main mistakes people make when thinking of the providential ways of God are these: first, that the power of the Holy Spirit is brought to bear on some situations and not on others; and second, that when it is brought to bear, it brings an *ad hoc* decision. We should know that God's will is not only for the elect, and that when it comes down the scale to us, it is just as much the expression of divine wisdom as ever it was. If there were one Holy Spirit for general councils and another for preparing a catechism class, we would have every excuse for not recognizing the will of God in our own small lives: the will of God would have shrunk almost to invisibility. Fortunately for us, the saints have no monopoly of the will of God. Where the saints have the advantage over us is that, being more ready to cooperate with it, they see it more often.

The second misconception is probably more common — partly because it is easier to think of the Holy Spirit acting as we would act, meeting an emergency with a snap decision, and partly because it is not at all easy to arrive at the right view of it without seeming to compromise free will. The exercise of tracing cause and effect is a hazardous one and, except in cases such as we have considered that relate to known fact, unprofitable. When we apply the process too minutely to our own past, we can become victims of delusion. But allowing for all these drawbacks, there is often good reason to look back and acknowledge the providential handling of what appeared at the time inexplicable or wasteful or disastrous.

Certainly there can be no danger of delusion in accepting present misfortunes, however unpromising they appear, as possible material for future good. You do not have to look only at the next life for the fruition; you can find some surprising reversals of misfortune even in this one. Job's experience was by no means unique. This is not to say that you must place all your trust in a miraculous switch; you must place all your trust in God. By trusting God to bring you through the immediate trial, you dispose your soul to future graces. The immediate is seldom, if ever, the end of the affair.

If, for instance, this book I am writing is rejected by the publisher, or if the manuscript is destroyed in a file, I shall be disappointed. But I shall know, assuming I keep my wits about me, that out of the thought that has been put into it, a new and better book may emerge. The disappointment will have been a necessary stage, part of the potential. Moreover, if there should be no end-product, and the last to be seen of the present work is a rejection slip or a little heap of ashes, nothing has been wasted. It does not mean that God never intended the book to be written in the first place, and was not helping with His will as page followed page. All it means is that one outcome has been exchanged for another, and that His will prefers this expression rather than that.

One person's blocked opportunity may liberate a hundred other people's opportunities — may even, at a different level, liberate some of his own. Our lives are so closely knit with the lives of others, and our own individual experiences are so related to one another, that to imagine we have exhausted our resources must always be wrong. The moment the potential has in fact run out will be the moment when God decides we must die. Until then, we are material on the move, and our movement is having repercussions of which we have not perhaps the faintest idea. It is this thought, the thought of mutual responsibility among the members of Christ's body, which should keep people from committing suicide. The only really dead end is the taking of one's own life.

Compare an oil-painting with a piece of tapestry. If the painter is displeased with one of his figures, he can scrape the canvas and paint in another; the original composition has remained; all that has happened is that one figure went wrong and had to be taken out. With the tapestry, it is a different business altogether. If the weaver is dissatisfied, he cannot take out a thread, much less a figure in the group, without affecting the rest of the composition. The weaver has to go on or begin again.

So long as we live, we are committed — committed to the past and the future, to other people and to God. Someone has said (and if nobody has, it is high time somebody did say) that "what you realize after you realize it is the important thing," and if a man does not follow up his realizations — does not see them as having been made real to him by God for the express purpose of eliciting an act of his own will — he would be better off realizing nothing.

The prayer "Come, Holy Spirit" shows us how the will of God is meant not only to touch every point of our lives from outside but to penetrate and, in the theological sense, "inform" every act of ours on the inside. The "face of the earth," which has to be renewed, is transformed from within. The apostle does not go about the world imposing God's will as he would pin a badge; he goes about the world so united with the will of God as to be able to kindle in others "the fire of God's love." He does not even go about proclaiming a law, unless it is the law of divine love, which is more a matter of exchange than of rules, but rather, by the help of God's grace, he tries to teach men to be "'truly wise and ever rejoice in His consolations, through Christ our Lord." When he has shown them what true wisdom consists in, where to find true consolations, and how to rejoice in them, he explains to them the rules they have to keep in order to express their service.

"If you love me, keep my commandments."[49] We will to love, but the only proof of our love is the will to obey. What love can there be without submission? So you may say that neither the will nor the love nor the law comes superimposed from without. Even the life of Christ, coming to us from the pages of the Gospel, is more of an inward than an outward reality. It is born in our souls by the grace of a sacrament and developed in us by the grace of prayer and other sacraments. The Christian life does not consist in committing to memory the historical events of the Gospel and re-enacting them; the Christian life consists, rather, in trying to enter into the mind of Christ and living accordingly. The essential Christian purpose is to come closer to the mystery of Christ's will and model our own human will to that divine pattern.

Such, then, is what we mean when we speak about Christ being our model. His words are for our direction; His acts are for our inspiration and, where possible, imitation; His will is for our

[49]John 14:15.

identification. "I live, now not I, but Christ lives in me."[50] Indeed, unless we try to reach out and understand something of the interior relationship between our Lord's will and the Father, between our Lord's will and human beings, between our Lord's will and the created world with all its material furnishings, it is difficult to see how we can in any true sense fulfill our Christian obligation. Without such an understanding, however elementary and (of necessity) incomplete, Christ's life means no more than a biography. It is true that His teaching provides us with a pattern of behavior, but the experience of Christian history seems to show that a pattern of behavior is not enough. Where Christianity has failed over the centuries is where human wills have refused to fit into the pattern, into the divine will. What is true of the Christian family at large is true of its individual members. When a man says by implication, "Christ lives, now not Christ, but I live instead of Him," he misses the whole point not only of Christ's life but of his own.

It comes to this, then — that if the Christian refuses to let himself get involved in the life of Christ (which means in the *will* of Christ for him and for the world), he cannot expect the pattern to do the work for him. For religion to become alive, its members must contribute. The members contribute in their degree what Christ contributes in His, which is to say that they must give. They must choose. They must orientate their lives with a specific end in view. The destination as well as the direction and power of movement are given: "I am the way and the truth and the life. No man comes to the Father but by me."[51]

[50]Gal. 2:20.
[51]John 14:6.

Here we can examine the material that is provided for the two-fold work proposed above, the work for the satisfactory execution of which we ask the Holy Spirit's help. The work is twofold because we look beyond our own personal sanctification ("send forth Thy Spirit and our hearts shall be created") to the evangelization and sanctification of mankind ("and Thou shalt renew the face of the earth"[52]). We have as means for the undertaking the Creed and the life and teaching of our Lord. The Church supplies aid with both certainty of interpretation and the graces of the sacraments. How, it might be thought by a visitor from another planet, can we possibly go wrong? Ideally speaking, there should be no discrepancy between man's Christian beliefs and his engagement in everyday life. But committed to a material world, and spinning out his mortality in time sequences, he is always more or less conscious of his failure here; he deviates from the course laid down.

"Faith," says Daniélou, "offers a vision of the world which embraces all things in the perspective of God's plan. God is at work in our midst; we are impelled to be His coworkers." Yes, but even with this vision and with this impulse, we are at best unprofitable workers. And sometimes hardly coworkers at all. Why do we limp in this service, the service which we know to be worthwhile and which cannot, of its very nature, ask more of us than we can bear to give? Surely it is because we have, again, never fully made our own the implications of the mystery of the Incarnation. If to us Christ were *really* the exemplar, really as compelling as He was, say, to Zacchaeus or Mary Magdalene or Paul, would we not accept faith's offer of "a vision of the world which embraces all things in the perspective of God's plan" and apply, day in and day out for the whole of our lives, the lessons of that vision?

[52]Cf. Ps. 103:30 (RSV = Ps. 104:30).

Back, then, to the wisdom of Bethlehem, Nazareth, Galilee, and Calvary. How does our surrender match its summons? First, there are the circumstances surrounding the Nativity: lack of comfort, signs of not being wanted by those who might have been expected to help, no guarantee that on the material side matters would improve, loneliness at being in a strange place, uncertainty about the return home. These are things everyone has experienced at one time or another, but the fact that they were experienced by the most important family in the history of man should draw our attention to the will that arranges them. We should be grateful for being in the authentic tradition. If we want to know what God thinks we are worth, we might do worse than reflect upon what He sends us. We know how the Holy Family stands in the Father's sight, and if we can find any share at all in the neglect they were allowed to suffer at the hands of their fellow human beings, we have reason to congratulate ourselves.

Moving from the infancy to the ministry, we find the same summons to faith. The natural is accounted for in the dimension of the supernatural. The riddle of human existence can be solved only by the Divine Wisdom who posed it, and when Wisdom itself assumes human life and explains how we are to proceed, the way is clear — but clear only to those who accept His terms. His terms are Himself. His terms are the Father's will, to which He, the Son, was obedient "even unto death."[53] Without faith in the validity of our Lord's claims — among them being the claim that He was the perfect fulfillment of the Father's will — a man is forced back upon the historical and the rational. Such a man can see that every now and again in our Lord's life, there was reasonable expectation of success: when discovered as a boy in the Temple, He showed

[53]Phil. 2:8.

promise of great things; on the shores of Tiberias, there was a move to make Him king; it was freely admitted that He spoke more convincingly than any of the leaders of His time; on Palm Sunday, there was a popular demonstration and He entered the capital in triumph. But from here onward, the way is by no means clear to the man without faith. If the historical is strained to the utmost in the story of the Resurrection, the rational fails completely.

Take the Passion itself, ending with the death that, to reason, means defeat and, to faith, the climax. Again, the lesson is that if we want to know the connection between God's will and suffering, we have only to look at who it was who took on the whole of God's will and who suffered more than anyone else in all history. Getting near to the mystery of the Son's Passion is like getting near to the mystery of the Father's will; there has to be the act of surrender. One single hour of suffering, taken as the will of God, does more for the soul than any amount of sensible devotion.

The demand of faith that the Passion makes of us is something more than the mere notional consent we give to the facts as revealed in the Gospels; the challenge is to our experience. In our own sufferings, such as they are, God's grace is inviting us to active participation with those of our Lord. One of the main obstacles to our doing this — to the voluntary act of uniting our trials with His — is that we cannot imagine how our pinprick pains can be of any use to Him. Nor can we imagine how the Second Person of the Blessed Trinity can be subject to the same sort of things that bother us. Until we have convinced ourselves of the truth that our Lord could feel depressed, could feel the force of temptation, could be disappointed in people whom He loved, we have missed one of the most significant lessons Christ came to teach. So as to win our experimental knowledge of His Passion, He puts His own experience at our disposal, and so that we should have more to learn of

His passion, we put our experience at His. Understood rightly, and not merely accepted as a doctrine, the Passion takes us to the very edge of human experience. Not all of us are called to follow as far as "If this chalice may not pass away but I must drink it, Thy will be done,"[54] and perhaps very few indeed to the point of "My God, my God, why hast Thou forsaken me?"[55] but the experience of Christ is there — for the sharing.

Always in the last analysis it is the mystery of faith. The Blessed Sacrament is called exactly that: *mysterium fidei*. The Passion, the ordering of the universe, human free will and the fore-knowledge of God, grace moving infallibly within an organization composed of ordinary human beings: *mysteria fidei*. Life, with its unending conflict between reason and faith, can find security only in acceptance. Those who think that reason has the last word go one way; those who cling to faith go another. Goodness knows what goes on in the mind of the rationalist, but are we to believe that in the mind of the man who chooses to walk by faith, the rationalist conclusion no longer presses? Of course it does. The difference lies in the choice, the firmness of the choice, and the fidelity with which the will abides by the choice. "We must have great faith," says Mouroux in his book *The Meaning of Man*, "if we are to arrive at the harmonious union of the world." Yes indeed, and we must also have great faith if we are to arrive at a harmonious union within ourselves.

A Spanish philosopher, Miguel de Unamuno, wrote a number of novels that had as their theme the struggle of human existence. Man, never quite sure of his convictions, drives himself desperate with his search for truth. But what qualifies is neither the

[54]Matt. 26:42.
[55]Matt. 27:46.

uncertainty nor the desperation but the unremitting quest for truth. More fancifully, it is suggested that just as the writer of fiction relies on his characters to put across his message, so God needs human beings as a medium for His revelation.

More fancifully still, Unamuno suggests that if the novelist can dream up people out of his own head and give them being, may not God be doing the same — may not we be simply God's dream? May not the whole of human existence be no more than what God happens to be dreaming? Theologians would probably have something to say about his idea (which makes the elemental instinct for survival express itself in man's most imperative prayer, "Dream us, O Lord"), but if you substitute *willing* for *dreaming*, you need not be so far out. If the concept that makes us issue from a divine reverie is disagreeable, there is nothing disagreeable about being deliberately created, by the all-wise will of God. Correspondingly, it is not for a deity to issue from the dreams of man, and this is what in effect takes place when a man defines his own private religion. Subjective religion, selecting and interpreting and changing back and forth, dreams up not only its own standards but also the nature of its own source.

Back, then, to the surrender of the human will and reason to divine will and reason. How to do it, where to find our practical, viable plan? Christ is the perfect exemplar, God and man, the divine will made actual, divine love made imitable.

Chapter 15

∞

Apostles of God's Will

If what our Lord did and suffered brings us nearer to doing and suffering in the name of the Father's will, what He preached and prayed should do the same. He had been foretold as "the man of sorrows and acquainted with grief."[56] The prophecy related to His interior life. But there were other prophecies that related to His exterior life, to His work and message. He was hailed Isaiah as "prince of peace,"[57] and seven centuries later by Zechariah, the father of John the Baptist, as "the Orient from on high" who would visit the world "to enlighten them that sit in darkness and in the shadow of death, to direct our feet into the way of peace."[58] So it is of first importance that we should know something about this peace He was to establish and this light He was to spread.

In our Lord's mission on earth, two elements stand out as surpassing all others: the work of redeeming mankind, and the work of founding His Church. This *was* the peace He had come to

[56]Isa. 53:3.
[57]Isa. 9:6.
[58]Luke 1:78-79.

bring; this *was* the light He had come to spread. It might be said that every recorded act of His, and every recorded sermon, bore upon one or other of these elements. Now, He has told us that we must learn of Him, that we must come to the Father by way of Him, that His is the peace which He alone can give and which the world cannot disturb, that His is the light without which man works in darkness. He is the shepherd, the vine, the word, the name by which miracles are worked and prayers heard.

Such richness of illustration and identification overwhelms us, and we start casting about for a formula that will express all our Lord's activities in one. Fortunately, there is no lack of texts that give us what we want. Our formula, differently phrased in different passages of the New Testament, contains the essential quality we have been considering throughout this book. "My meat is to do the will of Him that sent me," our Lord says at the well in Samaria, "that I may perfect His work."[59] "I seek not my own will," He says when He is attacked for making Himself equal to the Father, "but the will of Him that sent me."[60] He repeats this phrase almost word for word when asked for a sign, when asked for "true bread from heaven."[61] Our Lord was perfectly fulfilling the Messianic psalm that makes him say, "Behold, I come to do Thy will, O God."[62] The point we are trying to make here is simply that it was *by* doing the Father's will that Christ redeemed mankind and founded a Church. So that right at the end of His life, He was able to say, "It is finished: I have done the work which Thou gavest me to do."[63]

[59]John 4:34.
[60]John 5:30.
[61]John 6:32.
[62]Cf. Ps. 39:8-9 (RSV = Ps. 40:7-8).
[63]Cf. John 17:4; 19:30.

The Father had willed the redemption of man and the foundation of the Church. Inseparably united with the will of His Father, Christ knew that nothing of the Father's will was left to be done on earth; He could now continue the union in heaven.

So much for the relationship between our Lord's outward accomplishment and inward union. What has He to say about ours? The story is parallel, and again the texts are abundant. "Not everyone who says to me, 'Lord, Lord,' shall enter into the kingdom of heaven," Christ explains when pointing out that a tree is judged by its fruits, "but he who does the will of my Father who is in heaven."[64] The response has to be that of obedience, not that of emotion or habit or professional pride. The same demand for a deliberate choice, when superficial impulse may incline the other way, is stressed in the parable of the two sons, which ends with the question that a child of five would be able to answer: "Which of the two" — one of whom was all eagerness to work but did not, the other reluctant but finally obedient — "did the father's will?"[65] Again, there is that vivid scene given by St. Mark which shows our Lord so pressed with His work of preaching that Mary and some of His relations have to send messages to say they would like to speak to Him: "Who is my mother and my brethren? . . . Whosoever shall do the will of God, he is my brother and my sister and my mother."[66] Lastly, when He tells us how to pray, He insists that our disposition should be that of readiness to do God's will. Without "Thy will be done," there would seem to be little point in praying at all. With it, there is nothing that may not be prayed for, and no reason the prayer should ever stop.

[64]Matt. 7:21.
[65]Matt. 21:31.
[66]Mark 3:32, 35.

We could go through the letters of the New Testament, combing them for references to the necessity for surrender to the Father's will. "He who does the will of God," says St. John, "abides forever."[67] "That doing the will of God," we read in Hebrews, "you may receive the promise."[68] St. Paul to the Romans: "Be not conformed to this world, but be reformed in the newness of your mind, that you may prove what is the good and the acceptable and the perfect will of God."[69] "Not serving the eye," St. Paul warns the Ephesians, "but as servants of Christ doing the will of God from the heart."[70] He tells the Colossians how Epaphras is constantly praying for them that they "may stand perfect and full in all the will of God."[71] There is testimony everywhere you look: the early Church was fed on the will of God, the word of God, the law of God.

We accept all this, and indeed there is no getting away from it if we have any faith at all, but the difficulty for most of us is keeping it up — both keeping up the appreciation of the doctrine and the will to put the doctrine into effect. Our Lord saw this weakness in us when He said, "If you *continue* in my word, then shall you be my disciples indeed; and you shall know the truth and the truth shall make you free."[72] The idea of service carries with it the idea of perseverance. The connotation is not so immediate today as it used to be, because room-service and car-service and similar passing acts of service have brought along a new element, but certainly

[67]1 John 2:17.
[68]Heb. 10:36.
[69]Rom. 12:2.
[70]Eph. 6:6.
[71]Col. 4:12.
[72]John 8:31-32.

when we talk about the service of God, we do not think of something intermittent. If God's will is a constant living actuality, our response should follow suit.

Too many people imagine that in order to serve God generously, they must be living lives they do not like. This is a misconception that deters people from embarking upon such a service because they do not see themselves persevering indefinitely. These are the people who understand about the first half of the text just quoted but who have missed the point about the second. The reward of continuing in God's service is knowledge of the truth — the truth "which makes you free," not "which makes you miserable." Enjoying the liberty of the children of God, the soul enjoys life. There is a great difference between a life of self-sacrifice, which is the Christian ideal, and the life of self-torture, with which we often identify the Christian ideal.

God gives us our lives to lead, and it is ungracious of us if we hate every minute of those lives. As we have seen, God's will may (and on occasion must) involve suffering, loneliness, and boredom; but suffering, loneliness, and boredom are not designed to make up the whole of life. We are not meant to be in the flame from morning until night, and certainly we are not meant to congratulate ourselves if we are. We are told to "rejoice in the Lord . . . everywhere give thanks . . . make of our sacrifice a pleasing offering,"[73] which clearly we cannot do if we cannot associate God's will with peace and liberty but only with conflict and darkness. If it is true that "God's providence is my inheritance," then I have inherited peace. I cannot proclaim my trust in providence and at the same time deny my peace. It may not be the bland tranquility of rest that follows my surrender to the providence of God, but

[73]Phil. 3:1; 5:20; 4:18.

then I have not bargained for the smooth. It will be the tranquility of order, it will be beyond the reach of foreboding, and will rely upon foundations more sure than any I could lay by careful planning. And as such is something to be thankful for.

Which brings us to the question of gratitude. We have seen how God's will is inseparable from Himself. Consequently, it is true to say that we are receiving expressions of Him, evidences of Him, little private revelations of Him, if you like, at every turn. If this is so, ought we not to be giving thanks — if not all the time, at least as often as we can? In a superior sort of way, perhaps, we smile a superior sort of smile when nuns say *Deo gratias* every few minutes and at the slightest thing. But they are right to say it. Let it be hoped they mean it.

The slightest thing deserves gratitude. Without thinking, we rely upon God's providence from moment to moment, so to make a habit of thinking about it and giving thanks is bound to bring us closer to God. We depend upon God for the air we breathe, but who gives thanks for air? The habit of conforming to God's will and the habit of thanking for it go together. That is why we find the saints brimming over with gratitude about everything: they live in perpetual acknowledgment.

Consider the difference this must make to the life of prayer. Recollection becomes the more or less normal thing. Where before it was the pleasurable that elicited acts of gratitude, now it is the conformity that produces them. The question at this stage is not whether the particular circumstance is pleasurable or painful, but whether the will can rise to it and be grateful for it. Accordingly, with conformity to the providential plan as its foundation, prayer becomes not so much a series of acts as a state. The condition on which it operates is solely the will of God, and the will of God is in constant operation.

Whether such prayer is seen as receptive or cooperative, as contemplative or discursive, it makes for the habit of gratitude. The thankful realization that all things come from God becomes second nature and the reason for living. The air we breathe may be cold or foggy or damp, but what difference does that make? We cannot go on breathing without it.

∞

In the previous section, we have talked about perseverance, peace, gratitude, and prayer. In case the connection between these is not at once obvious, we will emphasize the truth that there exists in fact a very considerable link. You have only to put the qualities in reverse to see how instability, insecurity, ingratitude, and neglect of prayer must destroy the exchange between the soul and God. Not until final perseverance is rewarded, peace eternally established, and gratitude assumed into everlasting prayer before God's throne shall we fully appreciate the synthesis. But in the meantime, while engaged on this journey which paradoxically finds its term only in infinity, we can proceed in unity. What has been described as "the happening of the saints to their vision" can be anticipated even by us who are beginners.

∞

Hitherto we have dwelt upon aspects of peace and unity with regard to the soul. In the remaining pages, we can investigate peace and unity in their wider context. More important than our own selves is the human race, and questions that have to do with world order are not as academic and remote as they may seem when we read about them in the papers. We should know that because God's will is working in the world as well as in us, the condition of the world is our concern. No part of God's will is excluded from our interest, and the part that relates to the spread of Christ's peace is every Christian's responsibility.

From the first Christmas day, when the *Gloria in excelsis Deo* announced peace to men of goodwill, until April 11, 1963, when Pope John XXIII issued his encyclical letter *Pacem in terris* to the world, the message has been the same. And in the year of this writing, John's successor, Pope Paul VI, is working on his predecessor's legacy. The present-day version of the Christmas hymn is roughly this: peace results from the order implanted by God in the heart of man; it means peace with God, peace with fellowmen, peace with authority. Such is the main theme of *Pacem in terris*. Commentators in the press, non-Catholic as well as Catholic, seem agreed that the encyclical is one of the most moving documents of recent years. Moving to what? Not, if we are to judge by what has since happened in the world, to action.

The words of a holy religious leader may move the heart to tears, may even move the intellect to conviction, but unless they also move the will to take action, the situation remains where it was. This is where the individual can play his part, even if it remains a very small one. According to Pope John, peace radiates from the individual. "The world will never be the dwelling-place of peace," he says, "until peace has found a home in each and every man, until every man preserves within himself the order ordained by God to be preserved." Peace, like liberty and truth and the will of God itself, is not static but dynamic.

We, who by God's grace have "looked into the perfect law of liberty"[74] and found peace in Christ, owe an obligation toward the spread of truth and order. We may not sit still and imagine we have satisfied our responsibilities by offering some of our prayers at Mass

[74]Jas. 1:25.

for the intentions of the Holy Father. The world is moving, and the Church with it: "they must upward still and onward, who would keep abreast of Truth." Granted that the starting-off place is the human soul, there has to be a start. And how, when you really get down to it, is a start to be made — and in what direction?

First, we have to make ourselves familiar with the nature of what the Gospel is now being called upon to face. This need not involve an intensive course of study: it calls for conditioning our minds to the fact that there is an emergency in the world and that we may not evade it. Whether we like it or not, we are caught up in it. We can either allow ourselves to be caught up as leaves in a spiral of wind, or we can join the whirl and try to show that it is spinning around by the will of God and that Christ is at its center. It will be a question of orientation: am I thinking of other people's needs in regard to God, or am I thinking only of my own? Is the peace that God has designed for mankind receiving any sort of contribution from me, or do I think of peace as a personal commodity that is best safeguarded by my refusal to get mixed up with outside affairs? Surely what was meant by Pope John's *aggiornamento* was precisely this: the recognition that the will of God could be moving in a fast-changing society and that tradition must keep up with it. The implication is not that tradition must be sacrificed; on the contrary, the implication is that it should be made more use of — in the contemporary setting.

A man whose world is limited to his family and friends and the people whom he meets at his work might well object at this point that his horizons are too restricted for participation in world affairs. "If God had wanted me to extend the life of Christ in the contemporary setting, He would have placed me in a better position to do so. Either I would have been called to be a public-relations officer, or I would have been allowed the time and the talent to

147

study the question. As things are, I have as much as I can do to fulfill the obligations I learned as a child from the catechism. I am
too set in my ways to start modernizing and updating my religion
to suit the changing scene." The objection would be valid if the
demand were for a headlong plunge into the ecclesiastical arena.
But nobody is asking you to plunge into the ecclesiastical arena —
unless, of course, you happen to be an ecclesiastic, in which case
you are expected to make a highly professional performance in the
environment where God has placed you — but only to attend to
what is going on in your own arena and, if necessary, to widen its
boundaries. Nobody is asking you to concern yourself with public
relations, but it may well be God's will that you should give more
attention to perfecting your private relations. What is demanded
is a more planned and, given the right circumstances, a more ex-
tended, application of traditional Christianity.

Much in this will depend upon the God-given sphere of influence. To the foreign secretary of a sovereign nation, the opportunity
of furthering Christian ideals would be considerable; to someone
who is bedridden, it would be less so. But, as we shall see before
leaving the subject, there is no time in a person's life when the effort to impart the peace, truth, and life of Christ may be laid aside.
Pope John was careful to include the laity in the apostolic mission,
urging men and women to see their secular callings in a supernatural light and to direct their professional enterprise toward specifi-
cally Christian ends. *Pacem in terris* presents the Church as a unity,
and not as divided between the official and the unofficial. If in the
past there has been a gap between those responsible for the man-
agement and mechanism of the Church and those responsible for
accepting what they get, such a gap must be bridged. The members
of the Church are members of its mission: this was understood in
the early Church and is coming to be better understood today. But

there was a long period when it was not understood, and despite successive pontificates in our own time that have pointed to the original concept, there is always the danger of making artificial divisions in at least three of the Church's four essential marks.

Following the first recommendation — that we should convince ourselves of need and opportunity — must come the exhortation to do something about it. Relating how we behave to what we believe has never been our strong point as Christians. It might be said that it has never been anybody's strong point, whether Christian or not. True, but the member of Christ's Church has more support: laws, sacraments, doctrines — everything is laid down for him, and he gets the grace to pick it up and act on it. How, then, to cope with this dichotomy (keenly felt by St. Paul as he tells his friends in Rome, "I see another law in my members warring against the law in my mind"[75]) so that we come to be ruled by what we believe rather than what our fallen natures prompt us to? St. Paul gives the answer when he says that the only force strong enough to resolve the difficulty is "the grace of God by Christ our Lord."[76] When the human will has chosen the Father's will and is living it in the life of the Son, there is order in the soul and neither weakness nor passion has the final say.

It is this order that somehow or other has to be communicated to a disordered world. Having become ordered ourselves — our senses and emotions subject to reason and will, our reason and will subject to God — we have something to offer to a society in conflict. By operating as a whole human being, the mature person that God intends me to be, I can unite with other whole and mature human beings and work toward the wholeness and maturity of

[75]Rom. 7:23.
[76]Rom. 7:25.

149

mankind. Here is the synthesis of Christian faith and Christian action that results in peace, the peace envisaged by the *Gloria in excelsis* and *Pacem in terris* alike.

Very well, then — you are not a foreign minister, not a member of the administration, not a union leader, not a political broadcaster or a columnist. Measure it down to size, and make a realistic judgment of your powers as seen against the background of the life to which God has called you. Are you going to tell me that you see no warring elements in the environment that meets you in your work, in your home, in your social contacts? And, having admitted that such warring elements exist, are you going to tell me that you are utterly powerless in the cause of harmony? We are not talking now of how to effect the restoration of order — each case is unique and must call for the exercise of the practical judgment — but of why we must want to. Like us, other people are members of Christ's Body. There must be order in Christ's Body: the members must be subject to the Head and at one with each other. Otherwise the body is divided, which is what the world is today.

Without stepping out of his environment, every man must reduce division and promote order. Take someone in the teaching profession who is concerned about preserving Christian principles in a system of education that leaves them out of account. Is he to look the other way? Is he, without a protest, to choose some other career in which this conflict will not come up? Or someone in the medical profession who sees operations performed that are at variance with his Catholic conscience. Or a lawyer who sees injustice in much that he is supposed to be standing for. Or a religious who finds that the order or congregation to which he belongs is departing from its essential spirit. Or a boy or girl in school who believes the atmosphere of the place to constitute a threat to faith or morals. Are not all these people pledged to pursue the Christian ideal?

In every environment, there must be struggle and contradiction, and it is everyone's duty to make a bid for order. Christ's order is not always man's ("My peace I give unto you, not as the world gives"[77]), but it is always for Christ's followers to point to it. In an age when questions of marriage, race relations, total war, strikes, sex education, capital punishment, and compulsory state controls are live issues, it is important that we set our standards by the mind of Christ.

It might be thought that far from spreading harmony, such tactics as we talk about would be more likely to cause further friction. Here again is where *Pacem in terris* has an answer. "Peace is but an empty word if it does not rest upon [the] order that is founded upon truth, built on justice, nourished and animated by charity, and brought into effect under the auspices of freedom." Truth, justice, charity: these are as much Pope John's theme as they are the theme of the prophet Isaiah. Our encounter with others, whether they are coreligionists or not, is in charity and not in battle. A happier term than *encounter* is the now more popular one, *exchange*, suggesting a mutual opening up. Indeed, the whole ecumenical movement is conditioned by the readiness to explore, in the interests of peace and justice and truth, the minds of other people and to let other people explore ours. If charity is not the channel of this exchange, the exchange will not take place. Truth and justice will suffer.

"Human society as we here picture it," says Pope John again, "demands that men be guided by justice, that they respect the rights of others and do their duty." This is where freedom comes in to its own, because although there can be no true freedom where truth is not accepted, neither can there be true freedom where

[77]Cf. John 14:27.

there is religious intolerance. Charity must underlie our every attempt to evangelize, or our apostolate is no more than propaganda. "It [human society] demands too that they be animated by such love," the encyclical goes on, "as will make them feel the needs of others as their own, and induce them to share their goods with others, and to strive in the world to make all men alike heirs to the noblest of intellectual and spiritual values." The range of charity is as boundless here as it is in the Sermon on the Mount. The barricades are down, and liberty is now given a clear run. "For human society thrives on freedom, namely, on the use of means which are consistent with the dignity of its individual members, who, being endowed with reason, assume responsibility for their own actions."

St. Paul puts the case for the freedom which is born of charity when he says, "You are not under the law but under grace . . . love is the fulfillment of the law."[78]

Sin, by destroying charity, repudiates order and makes freedom impossible. Life in Christ is lost, and fallen man reverts to his fallen state. All this may seem doctrinaire and remote, but when we apply it to the will of God, it has particular relevance. What it amounts to is that sin shuts out the will of God, hinders its action in the world, imprisons man within himself, and lays such a crust of selfishness over his soul that the working of grace cannot be properly seen. The man who has chosen sin has chosen to accept as part of life the anomalies and contradictions that find no place in God's antecedent will: social injustice, scientific nihilism, immorality — these things are no longer negations to him. Love has so far died in him that the flaws and scars are assumed to be of little or no importance.

[78]Cf. Rom. 6:14; 13:10.

Lastly but more briefly (since this is what the whole of this book has been about, and repetition wearies), there is the contribution to the world's need that the individual soul can make in the way of prayer and penance. When we pray, we accept and praise God's will; when we accept our sufferings voluntarily, we praise God's will. For the evils of the world, there is no therapy like that of prayer and penance. We have this on the authority of our Lord Himself when He was talking to His disciples about exorcism.[79] The beauty of it is that while there may be doubt as to how we are to fulfill our obligation as apostles of peace and love, there is no such difficulty when it comes to the practice of prayer and penance. Knowing that such an apostolate is bound to benefit mankind, all we have to do is to get on with it. As our prayer deepens and as our resignation under trial becomes more purified, the scope of our apostolate will become more clear. It will be seen as something all-embracing because it will come from the heart that has Christ at its center. "We used to say that the mission field was on the map," wrote an American Methodist, Stanley Jones, "but now I know it is in the heart." Pope John would have agreed with him. This is truly ecumenical, truly the spirit of *aggiornamento*, truly a reconciliation.

After offering the bread and wine at Mass, the priest prays "for our salvation and that of the whole world." In the Christian concept, prayer is dynamic, and the salvation worked for is universal.

Looked at in its essential terms of fulfilling the will of God, religion should grow from being a part-time commitment to being a whole-time attitude of mind. The actual exercises of religion may be various, and the temperature in which they are carried out may fluctuate, but when the human will has identified itself with Him

[79]Matt. 17:14-20.

who wills all, then a man may confidently say, "I will now not I, but God wills in me."

Qui pro vobis et pro multis tradetur in remissione peccatorum. The blood of Christ does not stand still. Nor is it shed for the few. The Incarnation and Redemption were for all, and their work is still going on.

Hubert van Zeller

(1905-1984)

Dom Hubert van Zeller was born in 1905 of English parents in Alexandria, Egypt, where his father was in military service during the time when the country was a British protectorate. Van Zeller was educated privately until the age of nine, when he was sent for the remainder of his schooling to the Benedictine Abbey at Downside, England. Upon completing his education at the age of eighteen, he spent a year working at a Liverpool cotton firm before entering the novitiate at Downside in 1924. Unsettled and distracted by his school duties and desiring a more austere way of life, he struggled with his vocation at Downside for many years, even leaving for a brief period in the 1930s to enter the stricter Carthusian monastery at Parkminster.

After his return to Downside, van Zeller became more involved in giving retreats and in writing about spiritual matters. By the time of his death in 1984, he had written scores of books on prayer and spirituality, which won him a devoted readership throughout the English-speaking world. In addition to being a writer, van Zeller was a prolific and talented sculptor, whose works grace many churches and monasteries in Britain and in the United States.

Although a friend of Oxford-educated Catholic writers such as Ronald Knox and Evelyn Waugh, van Zeller once described his own writing about the Faith as an effort to use "the idiom of every day to urge people of every day to embark upon the spirituality of every day." Written with moving depth and simplicity, van Zeller's books should be read by all Christians seeking to pray and serve with greater fidelity in these difficult days.

∞

Sophia Institute Press®

Sophia Institute is a nonprofit institution that seeks to restore man's knowledge of eternal truth, including man's knowledge of his own nature, his relation to other persons, and his relation to God. Sophia Institute Press® serves this end in numerous ways: it publishes translations of foreign works to make them accessible for the first time to English-speaking readers; it brings out-of-print books back into print; and it publishes important new books that fulfill the ideals of Sophia Institute. These books afford readers a rich source of the enduring wisdom of mankind.

Sophia Institute Press® makes these high-quality books available to the general public by using advanced technology and by soliciting donations to subsidize its general publishing costs. Your generosity can help Sophia Institute Press® to provide the public with editions of works containing the enduring wisdom of the ages. Please send your tax-deductible contribution to the address below. We welcome your questions, comments, and suggestions.

For your free catalog, call:
Toll-free: 1-800-888-9344

Sophia Institute Press®
Box 5284 • Manchester, NH • 03108
www.sophiainstitute.com

Sophia Institute® is a tax-exempt institution as defined by the Internal Revenue Code, Section 501(c)(3). Tax I.D. 22-2548708.